Kaplan Publishing are constantly finding new ways to support students looking for exam success and our online resources really do add an extra dimension to your studies.

This book comes with free MyKaplan online resources so that you can study anytime, anywhere. **This free online resource is not sold separately and is included in the price of the book.**

Having purchased this book, you have access to the following online study materials:

CONTENT	AAT	
	Text	Kit
Electronic version of the book	✓	✓
Knowledge Check tests with instant answers	✓	
Mock assessments online	✓	✓
Material updates	✓	✓

How to access your online resources

Received this book as part of your Kaplan course?
If you have a MyKaplan account, your full online resources will be added automatically, in line with the information in your course confirmation email. If you've not used MyKaplan before, you'll be sent an activation email once your resources are ready.

Bought your book from Kaplan?
We'll automatically add your online resources to your MyKaplan account. If you've not used MyKaplan before, you'll be sent an activation email.

Bought your book from elsewhere?
Go to **www.mykaplan.co.uk/add-online-resources**
Enter the ISBN number found on the title page and back cover of this book.
Add the unique pass key number contained in the scratch panel below.
You may be required to enter additional information during this process to set up or confirm your account details.

This code can only be used once for the registration of this book online. This registration and your online content will expire when the examinations covered by this book have taken place. Please allow one hour from the time you submit your book details for us to process your request.

Please scratch the film to access your unique code.

Please be aware that this code is case-sensitive and you will need to include the dashes within the passcode, but not when entering the ISBN.

AAT

Q2022

Internal Accounting Systems and Controls (INAC)

EXAM KIT

This Study Text supports study for the following AAT qualifications:
AAT Level 4 Diploma in Professional Accounting
AAT Diploma in Professional Accounting at SCQF Level 8

AAT: INTERNAL ACCOUNTING SYSTEMS AND CONTROLS

British Library Cataloguing-in-Publication Data

A catalogue record for this book is available from the British Library.

Published by:

Kaplan Publishing UK

Unit 2 The Business Centre

Molly Millar's Lane

Wokingham

Berkshire

RG41 2QZ

ISBN: 978-1-83996-895-2

© Kaplan Financial Limited, 2024

Printed and bound in Great Britain

The text in this material and any others made available by any Kaplan Group company does not amount to advice on a particular matter and should not be taken as such. No reliance should be placed on the content as the basis for any investment or other decision or in connection with any advice given to third parties. Please consult your appropriate professional adviser as necessary. Kaplan Publishing Limited and all other Kaplan group companies expressly disclaim all liability to any person in respect of any losses or other claims, whether direct, indirect, incidental, consequential or otherwise arising in relation to the use of such materials.

All rights reserved. No part of this examination may be reproduced or transmitted in any form or by any means, electronic or mechanical, including photocopying, recording, or by any information storage and retrieval system, without prior permission from Kaplan Publishing.

This Product includes content from the International Auditing and Assurance Standards Board (IAASB) and the International Ethics Standards Board for Accountants (IESBA), published by the International Federation of Accountants (IFAC) in 2023 and is used with permission of IFAC.

CONTENTS

	Page
Unit specific information	P.4
Index to questions and answers	P.5
Exam technique	P.6
Kaplan's recommended revision approach	P.7

Case Study Information	1
Practice questions	3
Answers to practice questions	43
Mock assessment questions	95
Answers to mock assessment questions	115

Features in this revision kit

In addition to providing a wide ranging bank of real exam style questions, we have also included in this kit:

- Paper specific information and advice on exam technique.
- Our recommended approach to make your revision for this particular subject as effective as possible.

Live assessments: scenario and reference material

Pre-release scenario and reference material is made available on the AAT website before the real assessment. You should regularly/periodically review the AAT website to gain access to this prior to the real assessment.

The real assessment tasks will be based on the business included within the scenario and reference material. You should familiarise yourself with the business and how it operates before the assessment.

Reviewing the pre-release material in advance will help you consider which areas may be tested on the real exam day.

You will find a wealth of other resources to help you with your studies on the AAT website:

www.aat.org.uk/

Quality and accuracy are of the utmost importance to us so if you spot an error in any of our products, please send an email to mykaplanreporting@kaplan.com with full details.

Our Quality Co-ordinator will work with our technical team to verify the error and take action to ensure it is corrected in future editions.

UNIT SPECIFIC INFORMATION

THE EXAM

FORMAT OF THE ASSESSMENT

The assessment is divided into several standalone tasks which cover all of the learning outcomes and assessment criteria.

In any one assessment, students may not be assessed on all content, or on the full depth or breadth of a piece of content. The content assessed may change over time to ensure validity of assessment, but all assessment criteria will be tested over time.

The learning outcomes for this unit are as follows:

	Learning outcome	Weighting
1	Understand the role and responsibilities of the accounting function within an organisation	10%
2	Evaluate internal control systems	25%
3	Evaluate an organisation's accounting system and underpinning procedures	25%
4	Understand the impact of technology on accounting systems	15%
5	Recommend improvements to an organisation's accounting system	25%
	Total	100%

Time allowed

2 hours 30 minutes

PASS MARK

The pass mark is 70

 Always keep your eye on the clock and make sure you attempt all questions!

DETAILED SYLLABUS

The detailed syllabus and study guide written by the AAT can be found at:

www.aat.org.uk/

INDEX TO QUESTIONS AND ANSWERS

	Page number	
	Question	Answer
CASE STUDY INFORMATION	1	
ROLE AND RESPONSIBILITIES OF THE ACCOUNTING FUNCTION		
Questions 1 – 18	3	43
EVALUATE INTERNAL CONTROL SYSTEMS		
Questions 19 – 34	10	54
EVALUATE ACCOUNTING SYSTEMS AND PROCEDURES		
Questions 35 – 48	18	67
UNDERSTAND THE IMPACT OF TECHNOLOGY ON ACCOUNTING SYSTEMS		
Questions 49 – 57	31	79
RECOMMEND IMPROVEMENTS TO ACCOUNTING SYSTEMS		
Questions 58 – 67	34	85
MOCK ASSESSMENT		
Questions and answers	95	115

EXAM TECHNIQUE

- **Do not skip any of the material** in the syllabus.

- **Read each question** *very* carefully.

- **Double check your answer** before committing yourself to it.

- Answer **every** question – if you do not know an answer to a multiple-choice question or true/false question, you don't lose anything by guessing. Think carefully before you **guess**.

- If you are answering a multiple-choice question, **eliminate first those answers that you know are wrong**. Then choose the most appropriate answer from those that are left.

- **Don't panic** if you realise you've answered a question incorrectly. Getting one question wrong will not mean the difference between passing and failing.

Computer-based exams – tips

- Do not attempt a CBA until you have **completed all study material** relating to it.

- On the AAT website there is a CBA demonstration. It is **ESSENTIAL** that you attempt this before your real CBA. You will become familiar with how to move around the CBA screens and the way that questions are formatted, increasing your confidence and speed in the actual exam.

- Be sure you understand how to use the **software** before you start the exam. If in doubt, ask the assessment centre staff to explain it to you.

- Questions are **displayed on the screen** and answers are entered using keyboard and mouse. At the end of the exam, you are given a certificate showing the result you have achieved.

- In addition to the traditional multiple-choice question type, CBAs will also contain **other types of questions**, such as number entry questions, drag and drop, true/false, pick lists or drop down menus or hybrids of these.

- In some CBAs you will have to type in complete computations or written answers.

- You need to be sure you **know how to answer questions** of this type before you sit the exam, through practice.

KAPLAN'S RECOMMENDED REVISION APPROACH

QUESTION PRACTICE IS THE KEY TO SUCCESS

Success in professional examinations relies upon you acquiring a firm grasp of the required knowledge at the tuition phase. In order to be able to do the questions, knowledge is essential.

However, the difference between success and failure often hinges on your exam technique on the day and making the most of the revision phase of your studies.

The **Kaplan textbook** is the starting point, designed to provide the underpinning knowledge to tackle all questions. However, in the revision phase, poring over text books is not the answer.

Kaplan pocket notes are designed to help you quickly revise a topic area; however, you then need to practice questions. There is a need to progress to exam style questions as soon as possible and to tie your exam technique and technical knowledge together.

The importance of question practice cannot be overemphasised.

The recommended approach below is designed by expert tutors in the field, in conjunction with their knowledge of the examiner and the specimen assessment.

You need to practise as many questions as possible in the time you have left.

OUR AIM

Our aim is to get you to the stage where you can attempt exam questions confidently, to time, in a closed book environment, with no supplementary help (i.e. to simulate the real examination experience).

Practising your exam technique is also vitally important for you to assess your progress and identify areas of weakness that may need more attention in the final run up to the examination.

In order to achieve this we recognise that initially you may feel the need to practice some questions with open book help.

Good exam technique is vital.

THE KAPLAN REVISION PLAN

Stage 1: Assess areas of strengths and weaknesses

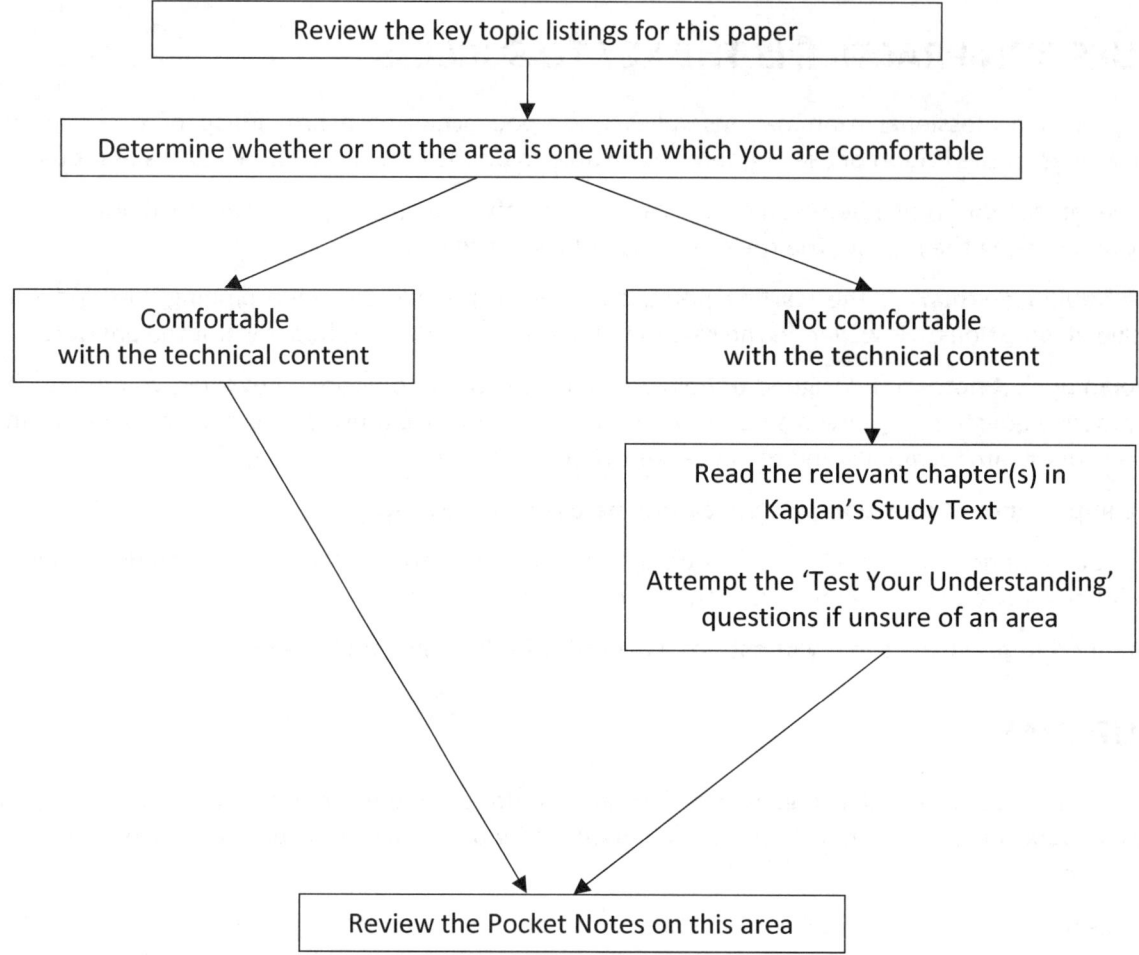

Stage 2: Practice questions

Follow the order of revision of topics as presented in this kit and attempt the questions in the order suggested.

Try to avoid referring to text books and notes and the model answer until you have completed your attempt.

Review your attempt with the model answer and assess how much of the answer you achieved.

Stage 3: Final pre-exam revision

We recommend that you **attempt at least one 2 hour 30 minute mock examination** containing a set of previously unseen exam standard questions.

Attempt the mock CBA online in timed, closed book conditions to simulate the real exam experience.

Section 1

CASE STUDY INFORMATION

This case study contains a scenario which is referred to within various questions within this exam kit.

Scenario

This information is based on the scenario of Healthyou Ltd (Healthyou).

Healthyou is a private limited company, based in Harrogate, which operates a small number of shops across the north of England selling health supplements. Its approach is to use only organic products approved for human consumption by the food standards regulator.

Company background

History

The business was started 15 years ago by Sam Shah and Pat Singh when they opened their first shop in Harrogate. Although the early years of the business were quite difficult, the trend towards individuals taking more responsibility for their health and wellbeing has boosted the popularity and use of health supplements. This has resulted in a dramatic rise in both sales and profits over the last four years.

This surge in popularity, and significantly improved operational performance, has led to a further ten shops opening across the north of England during the last three years. The shop locations are selected based upon age, income and employment demographics. The intention is to open another four shops in the next financial year.

From the beginning, Healthyou has always been focused on providing a wide range of health supplements to relieve a variety of ailments, particularly relating to exercise-related issues such as sore and tight muscles. This has proved to be an important part of the success of the business, with gym members and runners being a large proportion of its customers.

Recent developments

Last year, Healthyou decided to expand its product offering by allowing customers to order products online. The products can be purchased and ordered using 'click-and-collect' at a nominated store, or for a small additional charge, be delivered directly to the customer. Due to logistical issues with deliveries, the 'click-and-collect' service is currently only available from two of the shops. The online service has been a success, but has resulted in a 5% reduction in the number of customers purchasing products in shops since the online service was introduced.

The expansion of Healthyou into multiple shops has meant that additional staff have had to be recruited to manage this increased operational activity. Healthyou has also had to rent premises in Harrogate to act as the business's head office.

Resources

On 31 December 20X4, Healthyou had 78 employees.

Department	Number of staff
Purchasing	7
Storage and distribution	12
Retail	42
Marketing and development	6
Administration	11

Staff

Some of Healthyou's key personnel are listed below:

Managing Director	Sam Shah
Deputy Managing Director	Pat Singh
Finance Director	Yoshika Mane
Human Resources Director	Pat Smythe
Regional Operations Manager	Jun Khan
Commercial Manager	Clem Seddon
Financial Controller	Ping Alonso
Purchasing Manager	Kazu Kumar
Development Chef	Hiromi Patel
Accounts Payable Manager	Kyo Suarez
Accounts Payable Clerk	Bai Firminio
General Accounts Clerk	Setsuna Reina
Cashier	Daya Haaland
Payroll Manager	Zhong Salah

Sustainability

The business has always prided itself on being a good employer, supporting local suppliers and minimising its environmental impact. As the business grows, the challenge is to make sure those principles stay embedded within the business. This includes:

- minimal waste within its activities. All packaging such as cardboard, paper and plastic is recyclable.
- minimum hourly rate of £12.50 per hour for all staff, to be constantly reviewed and kept ahead of the national minimum living wage.
- offering customers the facility to bring their own containers to fill with, reducing the need for packaging (e.g. cereals).

Section 2

PRACTICE QUESTIONS

ROLE AND RESPONSIBILITIES OF THE ACCOUNTING FUNCTION

THE ACCOUNTING FUNCTION

1 ETHICS

Which statement provides a definition of business ethics?

	✓
Business ethics is concerned with complying with the law in business situations.	
Business ethics is concerned with complying with the law and all relevant accounting regulations.	
Business ethics is concerned with making the most appropriate moral judgements in business situations.	
Business ethics is concerned with avoiding illegal transactions in business situations.	

2 GOOD ETHICAL BEHAVIOUR

Which TWO statements are key features of good ethical behaviour?

	✓
Good ethical behaviour increases costs without any significant benefits to the organisation.	
Good ethical behaviour helps to enhance the reputation of the organisation.	
Good ethical behaviour helps to reduce the risk of problems arising in the organisation.	
Good ethical behaviour may result in an organisation becoming uncompetitive.	

3 IMPORTANCE OF ETHICS

Why is good ethical behaviour within the accounting function important?

	✓
It ensures that the business will make a profit on its trading activities.	
It ensures that employees in the accounting function will not make errors when performing their work.	
It guarantees that the accounting records do not contain any errors omissions or misstatements.	
It helps to maintain the accuracy and reliability of the accounting records.	

4 SUSTAINABILITY

Which statement provides a definition of sustainability?

	✓
Sustainability is defined as minimising the financial cost of inputs to produce the required products and services.	
Sustainability is defined as meeting the needs of the present whilst minimising any adverse impact upon future generations to meet their own needs.	
Sustainability is defined as minimising waste and pollution when producing goods and services.	
Sustainability is defined as the business being able to continue in existence for as long as possible.	

5 GOOD SUSTAINABILITY PRACTICES

Which TWO of the following are good sustainability practices within the accounting function?

	✓
Having a paperless office, with employees using accounting software and email communication to do their work.	
Purchasing plastic office furniture as it is cheaper than wood and likely to last longer.	
Not installing double glazing on the office windows.	
Using video conferencing for meetings, rather than employees travelling to meet in person.	

6 IMPORTANCE OF SUSTAINABILITY

Which TWO statements identify why an organisation should have good sustainability policies and practices?

	✓
Good sustainability policies and practices will ensure that the organisation will make a profit on its trading activities.	
Good sustainability policies and practices will always result in choosing the lowest cost when purchasing materials and other business inputs.	
Good sustainability policies and practices help to improve the long-term viability of the organisation.	
Good sustainability policies and practices help to maintain and improve the reputation of the organisation.	

7 STAFF STRUCTURES I

Identify whether each of the following statements is true or false.

	True ✓	False ✓
A multinational organisation is likely to have a longer scalar chain than a single-site organisation.		
A 'flat' organisation will have a long scalar chain.		
A manager in a 'flat' organisation will always have a narrower span of control than a manager in a 'tall' organisation.		
A manager's span of control may include employees who work in different departments or in different locations.		

8 STAFF STRUCTURES II

Identify whether the following statements about a broad span of control are true or false.

	True ✓	False ✓
It improves productivity for the organisation.		
It has fewer levels of management.		
It is less expensive to operate.		
Employees can easily give feedback to managers on ways to improve systems.		

AAT: INTERNAL ACCOUNTING SYSTEMS AND CONTROLS

FINANCIAL INFORMATION USED BY STAKEHOLDERS

9 FINANCIAL INFORMATION I

Complete the following statements relating to financial information.

Monthly or quarterly accounts are normally prepared for the benefit of (GAP 1). These accounts help them to make decisions regarding (GAP 2).

Picklist: GAP 1 business owners, potential investors, managers

Picklist: GAP 2 whether or not to invest in the business, controlling and managing the business

10 ACCOUNTS PRODUCED BY MANAGERS

State whether the following statements are true or false.

	True / False
The form and content of accounts produced by managers for decision-making and control purposes must comply with the law and with relevant accounting standards.	
Annual financial statements will contain exactly the same information as accounts produced by managers for decision-making and control purposes.	

11 FINANCIAL STATEMENTS I

Select which financial statement would enable a user to identify the information described.

	Financial statement
The amount of cash paid to purchase property, plant and equipment during the year.	
The amount of trade payables at the year end.	
By how much the cash and equivalents balance has increased or decreased during the year.	
Whether or not land and buildings were revalued during the year.	

Picklist: Statement of profit or loss, Statement of financial position, Statement of cash flows, Statement of changes in equity

Note: each statement may be used more than once within the table above.

12 FINANCIAL STATEMENTS II

State which financial statement will be used to identify information for the calculation of the following accounting ratios.

	Financial statement
Gearing ratio.	
Gross profit margin.	
Current ratio.	

Picklist: Statement of profit or loss, Statement of financial position, Statement of cash flows, Statement of changes in equity

13 CEEDEE LTD

Ceedee Ltd is a manufacturing company that uses a computer software package to record and process accounting transactions. The computer software package also produces periodic management accounts and annual financial accounts.

State whether or not each of the following situations would require Ceedee Ltd to make changes within its existing accounting systems.

	Change systems / No change
The directors decided to change the depreciation rate applicable to delivery vans.	
The recruitment of a new accounts clerk in the accounts department.	
The issue of an updated accounting standard dealing with the valuation of inventory.	

14 FINANCIAL INFORMATION II

State whether the following statements are true or false.

	True / False
Accounting information produced to assist decision making by managers is likely to be more detailed than the annual financial statements.	
Annual financial statements contain all information that an external stakeholder would possibly need to make fully informed decisions.	

15 PERFORMANCE INDICATORS

Identify the relevant component required as part of the calculation for each of the following performance indicators

Current ratio.	Gap 1
Inventory turnover.	Gap 2
Trade receivables collection period.	Gap 3
Return on capital employed.	Gap 4

Gap 1	✓
Total current assets	
Cost of sales	
Operating profit	
Revenue	

Gap 2	✓
Total current assets	
Cost of sales	
Operating profit	
Revenue	

Gap 3	✓
Total current assets	
Cost of sales	
Operating profit	
Revenue	

Gap 4	✓
Total current assets	
Cost of sales	
Operating profit	
Revenue	

16 FINANCIAL INFORMATION III

Identify whether the following statements about financial information are true or false.

	True / False
The budgetary control report is presented to the board of directors.	
The statement of financial position is used to determine the liquidity of an organisation.	

CHANGES TO MANAGEMENT INFORMATION

17 MANAGEMENT INFORMATION SYSTEMS I

State whether the following statements are true or false.

	True / False
It is not necessary for the management information system to distinguish between cash and credit sales when calculating the trade receivables collection period.	
If the management information system is able to classify liabilities as either current liabilities or non-current liabilities, this provides useful financial information for both internal and external stakeholders.	

18 MANAGEMENT INFORMATION SYSTEMS II

Complete the following statements relating to management information systems.

When an organisation changes its strategic objectives, it (GAP 1) require changes to its management information system. It is important that the management information system (GAP 2) change to meet the needs of internal stakeholders.

Picklist: GAP 1 will, will not

Picklist: GAP 2 does, does not

EVALUATE INTERNAL CONTROL SYSTEMS

INTERNAL CONTROLS

19 ORGANISATION SIZE

State whether the following statements are true or false.

	True / False
A small organisation does not need to have any internal controls.	
The accounting records in a large organisation which applies a range of effective internal controls in the accounting system will be guaranteed to be free from error.	
An online retailer can apply a range of effective internal controls within its accounting software systems.	

20 TYPES OF INTERNAL CONTROL

Match the type of internal control with each of the control examples noted below.

	Type of control
An organisation operates a smartcard system with a barrier that prevents visitors accessing the building (other than reception area).	
As part of the selection and recruitment process, an organisation requires that applicants undergo an aptitude test and provide confirmation of their academic qualifications.	
Within the accounts department of an organisation, Huan is responsible for recording cash receipts from credit customers, Kiran is responsible for updating the sales/receivables ledger accounts and Nilam performs the monthly reconciliation of the sales/receivables ledger control account with the total of the sales/receivables ledger balances.	

Picklist: Authorisation and approval, Arithmetic and accounting, Supervision, Segregation of duties, Organisational, Physical, Personnel, Management

21 TYPES OF INTERNAL CONTROL

Match the type of internal control with each of the control examples noted below.

	Type of control
An organisation requires that the purchase of any items of equipment which cost £500 or more is agreed in advance by a senior manager before the purchase is made.	
When starting a new job, Guang was presented with a job description which specified individual responsibilities and identified the departmental manager to contact if there were any work-related problems.	
Within the accounting and finance department of an organisation, Akira oversees the work of a new member of staff and is able to offer practical guidance and instruction to ensure that transactions are processed correctly.	

Picklist: Authorisation and approval, Arithmetic and accounting, Supervision, Segregation of duties, Organisational, Physical, Personnel, Management

22 EFFECTIVE INTERNAL CONTROLS

State whether the following statements are true or false.

	True ✓	False ✓
If a large multi-site organisation has comprehensive authorisation and approval procedures for transactions, along with effective segregation of duties in the accounting and finance department, it will still need a range of other internal controls to help manage organisational activities effectively.		
An effective internal control system will prevent any fraud or error from occurring.		
In a small company with two directors and two employees in the accounting department it is still possible to have effective supervision and authorisation and approval controls in place.		

AAT: INTERNAL ACCOUNTING SYSTEMS AND CONTROLS

23 RESPONSIBILITY FOR THE INTERNAL CONTROL SYSTEM

Within an organisation, who is responsible for ensuring that it has an effective system of internal controls?

	✓
The external auditor.	
The internal auditor.	
The board of directors.	
The finance director only.	

24 INTERNAL CONTROLS I

An internal control system in an organisation consists of five components: the control environment, the risk assessment process, the information system, control activities and monitoring of controls.

Match each of the following activities to the component that it illustrates.

	Control environment ✓	Information system ✓	Control activities ✓
Communication and enforcement of integrity and ethical values.			
A requirement that all payments in excess of £1,000 require approval from two directors.			
The preparation of monthly management accounts.			

25 INTERNAL CONTROLS II

Healthyou is looking at introducing new internal controls to help reduce the risk of fraud.

Match each of the following activities to the type of control that it illustrates.

	Authorisation and approval ✓	Arithmetical and accounting ✓	Physical control ✓
The purchase/payables ledger control clerk produces a reconciliation of the ledger account balances with the total on the payables ledger control account every month.			
The petty cash float is kept in a locked box within a safe when not required.			
The chief accountant extracts a trial balance from the ledger accounts before preparing the annual accounts.			

26 INTERNAL CONTROLS III

Indicate whether the following limitations are true or false.

	True	False
If the costs of implementing a particular control exceed the benefits to be gained from its application, a business is unlikely to apply that control.		
The effectiveness of many controls do not rely upon the honesty and integrity of individuals applying them.		
Internal controls apply to all items, irrespective of their value.		
Standard controls are designed to deal with every possible transaction, no matter how unusual.		

27 INTERNAL CONTROLS IV

Sam Shah, Managing Director, is concerned that the business does not have a strong system of internal controls and has made suggestions for improvements to the current system. You have been asked to match the internal controls to the weakness that has been identified.

Identify which control is suitable for each of the following weaknesses.

Weaknesses	Control
Theft of inventory from an open warehouse.	Gap 1
Purchase orders are sent to suppliers without attaching a Purchase Order number.	Gap 2
Entry of a one-off transaction into the accounting system.	Gap 3
Supplier accounts are managed and paid by the same person.	Gap 4
Incorrect entry of sales invoices into the sales daybook.	Gap 5
Non-compliance with appropriate accounting regulations and standards resulting from lack Of CPD.	Gap 6

Options	Gap No.
Management controls	
Segregation of duties	
Check arithmetical accuracy	
Physical access controls	
Authorisation and approval	
Competent personnel	

28 SMALL OR LARGE

As Healthyou has been expanding, you are reviewing its current internal controls and assessing their suitability as the company continues to develop and grow. Some new members of the management team have recently completed a management training course, where they were told that the type of internal controls needed depended on the size of the organisation in which they were used.

Identify whether the following internal controls are more suitable for a small or a large organisation.

Internal control	Small	Large
Monthly inventory checks.		
Segregation of duties for the posting of purchase invoices, credit notes, preparing a supplier payment list and making payments to suppliers.		
All purchase orders must be authorised by the Managing Director.		

PREVENT AND DETECT FRAUD AND SYSTEMIC WEAKNESS

29 FRAUD I

A clothes store in the city centre is trying to minimise the risk of clothes being stolen by shoppers.

Which TWO of the following would best reduce the risk of clothes being stolen from the store?

	✓
Segregation of duties between customer service staff on the shop floor and other members of staff taking payments from customers at tills.	
Requiring that all goods purchased are paid for by credit card or debit card, rather than cash.	
Each item of clothing has a security tag attached which can only be removed by a member of staff when the customer pays for the goods.	
In-store security guards and cameras monitor shoppers, particularly as they are leaving the store.	

30 FRAUD II

The financial accountant of Onyx Ltd is concerned about the risk of fictitious overtime claims by employees.

Which TWO of the following control activities would best prevent this issue occurring?

	✓
The total cost of the payroll for the current month is compared with the total payroll cost for the previous month.	
All overtime claims must be reviewed and authorised by a manager prior to processing any payment.	
Review of working hours logged (e.g. by clock card, swipe card etc) by a responsible person.	
Supervision of the wages pay out by an independent official.	

31 FRAUD III

State whether the following statements are true or false.

	True	False
Fraud normally happens when someone has seen an opportunity, a weakness in the company's systems, and believes that the potential rewards will not outweigh the risk of being caught.		
The three prerequisites for fraud to occur are opportunity, motivation and honesty.		
Fraud investigations can often reveal a high level of inventory losses or unauthorised amounts written off to the sales/receivables ledger.		

32 SYSTEMIC WEAKNESS

This task is about the types of fraud in the workplace combined with ways in which it can be detected and prevented.

Pat Singh, Healthyou's Deputy Managing Director, is concerned about the suitability of the internal controls and has identified the following weaknesses. You have been asked to explain why these weaknesses may have occurred.

Identify the cause of the following weaknesses:

Weaknesses	Cause
Segregation of duties is deemed unnecessary.	Option 1
Management and supervision are based remotely.	Option 2
Staff create their own spreadsheets to prepare month-end reports instead of using Healthyou's accounting software.	Option 3
Inventory counts are rarely done.	Option 4

Option 1	✓
Lack of monitoring	
Lack of controls	
Lack of leadership	
Poor implementation of controls	

Option 2	✓
Lack of monitoring	
Lack of controls	
Lack of leadership	
Poor implementation of controls	

Option 3	✓
Lack of monitoring	
Lack of controls	
Lack of leadership	
Poor implementation of controls	

Option 4	✓
Lack of monitoring	
Lack of controls	
Lack of leadership	
Poor implementation of controls	

33 FRAUD IV

A construction company found that certain employees were bypassing the approval process for ordering building materials, leading to an overstock and eventual write-offs. Site managers are always available on-site in case employees need any assistance.

Complete the following statements.

The financial statement area under scrutiny was (GAP 1), where there was clear (GAP 2).

The company has now mandated (GAP 3) to track orders effectively. This aims to enhance the integrity of the (GAP 4) reported.

Picklist: GAP 1 trade payables, inventories, revenue

Picklist: GAP 2 lack of controls, lack of leadership, lack of monitoring

Picklist: GAP 3 sequential purchase order numbering, an open-door policy with management, extended training of staff

Picklist: GAP 4 assets, income, equity

34 TYPES OF FRAUD

Identify whether the following are an example of non-financial or financial fraud.

	Non-financial	Financial
An employee falsified their qualifications and experience on their CV to secure a job role.		
A cashier in a retail outlet deliberately under-scanned sales through the checkout, to allow friends to purchase items at a reduced price.		
Inventory theft from a central warehouse by delivery staff.		

EVALUATE ACCOUNTING SYSTEMS AND PROCEDURES

EFFECTIVENESS OF THE ACCOUNTING SYSTEM

35 PURCHASE CYCLE CONTROLS I

Healthyou has experienced occasions when payment was made for goods not received.

Which TWO of the following controls in a purchase cycle could be implemented to reduce the risk of payment of goods not received?

	✓
Sequentially pre-numbered purchase requisitions and sequence check.	
Matching of goods received note with purchase invoice.	
Goods are inspected for condition and quantity and agreed to purchase order before acceptance.	
Daily update of inventory system.	

36 PURCHASE CYCLE CONTROLS II

Healthyou has experienced occasions when unnecessary goods and services were purchased.

Which TWO of the following controls in the purchase cycle could be implemented to reduce the risk of procurement of unnecessary goods and services?

	✓
Centralised purchasing department.	
Sequentially pre-numbered purchase requisitions and sequence check.	
Orders can only be placed with suppliers from the approved suppliers list.	
All purchase requisitions are signed as authorised by an appropriate manager.	

PRACTICE QUESTIONS: SECTION 2

37 EXPENSE CLAIM CONTROLS

Kim Ono has been appointed as the new IT manager at Healthyou and really enjoys the job. The remuneration is not great, and other managers at the company have explained the way they 'get around' that issue. The sales manager explains to Kim that the key is to 'put everything on expenses – private petrol, drinks and even clothing. It's all fine and as long as you have a receipt, no one in the finance department will question it' and continues by saying 'It's fine because the board are aware of it and turn a blind eye'.

Which ONE of the following essential internal control measures is evidently missing?

	✓
Healthyou lacks a control environment as the board are not setting an ethical tone at the top.	
Healthyou lacks an Internal Audit department.	
Healthyou lacks an experienced finance manager.	
Healthyou lacks an external auditor.	

38 HEALTHYOU – INVENTORY COUNTING PROCESSES

Each winter, Healthyou is obliged to count its inventory. This is typically done on the morning of 1 January.

For this business, inventory is held in a number of different places. Each location typically carries a range of products, including some goods received when customers have used the 'click-and-collect' service. Due to their nature, some products have a short use-by date and must be kept in a chiller cabinet.

Each shop manager organises the inventory count at their own location using their permanent staff. In addition, this year, Healthyou arranged for an internal auditor to attend some of the inventory counts and feedback their findings. It was hoped that this would lead to improved procedures in the future. At one location, the local staff were low on numbers and so the internal auditor acted as a counter and an auditor at the same time.

The count at each location was organised into two teams. The first would count goods on the shop shelves and chiller cabinet, and the second in the back stores area.

For each location, sales information is detailed enough for head office to prepare pre-printed inventory sheets showing expected inventory levels for most products, so staff are expected to count these items and tick the relevant box if quantities match. Where there is a disagreement, the revised quantity should be added.

For the remaining products, such as fresh goods and health snacks, sales information does not allow head office to calculate exactly what quantities should be present. For these products a sheet of all possible products is generated and staff are expected to complete the quantities.

Suppliers were requested not to deliver during the inventory counts. This policy was mostly followed, but one supplier did make a delivery to three locations during the count. The drivers offloaded the items outside the store so as not to interfere with the counting process.

During the count, boxes of health drinks not yet unpacked were not opened but the slips on the side of the boxes were used to note the contents on the inventory sheets.

Goods were not individually checked for best before or use-by dates, but staff were asked to make a note of any items that looked past their best.

Outline 3 weaknesses and their effect on the accounting systems in the boxes below:

Weakness	Effect of Weakness

39 BANK RECONCILIATION

Which ONE of the following statements explains the purpose of a bank reconciliation?

	✓
It is a control to ensure that the bank statement balance as at the end of the accounting year is correct.	
It is a control to ensure that all payments required have been made.	
It is a control to minimise the risk of errors and omissions in the cashbook, and to identify such items for further investigation.	
It is a control to ensure that all unrecorded receipts are identified and recorded in the cashbook.	

PRACTICE QUESTIONS: SECTION 2

40 RECEIVABLES LEDGER CONTROL ACCOUNT RECONCILIATION

Which ONE of the following statements explains the purpose of the reconciliation of the trade receivables control account?

	✓
It is a control to ensure that receipts from credit customers have been accounted for.	
It is a control to ensure that invoices raised relating to credit customers have been accounted for.	
It is a control to ensure that entries in the control account agree with the total of the receivables ledger, which guarantees that there are no errors or omissions in either the control account or the ledger account balances.	
It is a control to ensure that entries in the control account agree with the total of the receivables ledger. Even if that's the case, the control account and/or ledger account balances may still contain errors or omissions.	✓

41 HERBUS SALES AND DESPATCH SYSTEM

The Board of Healthyou is considering buying a business that grows herbs and plants used for medicinal purposes. One potential target identified is Herbus, which sells its produce to a range of retail and other outlets, such as health clubs and to the end consumer. Herbus has a dedicated sales team to manage the relationship with larger customers. Orders from smaller business customers and the public are mainly placed through Herbus' website, while some are also made via telephone.

Clem Seddon (Commercial Manager) has started to investigate the farm in more detail and has some concerns over its sales and despatch system. Clem is reasonably happy over the way sales to major customers are dealt with but has concerns over telephone and website transactions.

Online orders are automatically checked against inventory records and herb-picking schedules for availability; telephone orders, however, are checked manually by order clerks after the call. A follow-up call is usually made to customers if there is insufficient inventory. When taking telephone orders, clerks note down the details on plain paper and afterwards they complete a three-part pre-printed order form. These order forms are not sequentially numbered and are sent manually to both despatch and the accounts department.

As Herbus is expanding, customers are able to place online orders which will exceed their agreed credit limit by 10%. Online orders are automatically forwarded to the despatch and accounts department.

A daily pick list is printed by the despatch department and this is used by the warehouse team to despatch goods. The goods are accompanied by a despatch note and all customers are required to sign a copy of this. On return, the signed despatch notes are given to the warehouse team to file.

Sales invoices are created using the sales quantities from the despatch notes and the authorised sales prices which are programmed into the invoicing system. If a discount has been given, e.g. for a bulk order, then this has to be manually entered by the sales clerk onto the invoice.

AAT: INTERNAL ACCOUNTING SYSTEMS AND CONTROLS

Due to the expansion of the company and the associated increase in the number of sale invoices, extra accounts staff have been asked to help out temporarily with producing the sales invoices. Normally it is only two sales clerks who produce the sales invoices.

Identify and explain FIVE deficiencies in Herbus' sales and despatch system and evaluate the impact of these deficiencies.

Deficiency	Evaluation of impact

42 PAYROLL FRAUD

You have identified that the payroll clerk, Kim Mackie, has been overpaying themselves by £400 each month for the past three months. You have also detected that for nine months Kim has been paying someone else (named Scott Bennett) an annual salary of £30,000. Scott is not an employee of the business and has no payroll records or payslips.

Identify which of the following procedures would detect the frauds identified above.

Procedures	Would detect ✓	Would not detect ✓
The Financial Controller performs a numerical accuracy check of all payslips.		
An online portal is used to send payslips directly to employees. A paper copy is not posted out to employees' home addresses.		
The payment list is prepared by Kim. Prior to any payment being made, this is reviewed, checked and authorised by the Financial Controller.		
Zhong Salah (Payroll Manager) completes a check that ensures that all employees are paid (at least) the minimum wage.		
A wages control account is not maintained.		
Payslips are always prepared by Kim. These are then checked against bank payments by the Financial Controller.		

43 HEALTHYOU'S GENERAL LEDGER SYSTEM

The general ledger of Healthyou is controlled by Yoshika Mane (Finance Director) and Ping Alonso (Financial Controller) with both of these people able to make independent journal entries. Yoshika and Ping are friends and keen snowboarders and skaters who like to get away over the winter period to snowboard and skate in various parts of the world. This isn't always easy to arrange as the year-end work needs to finish quickly to enable this holiday to take place. Pat Smythe (HR Director) is given access to the general ledger over this period in the unlikely event further adjustments are needed.

Ping or Yoshika do not review each other's journal entries, as there is considerable trust between the two individuals.

Anyone with general ledger access can create new general ledger accounts.

Non-current assets accounting policy

During the current year, the approach taken to accounting for non-current assets has been investigated by Yoshika. Having compared the approach taken by Healthyou to other similar businesses, Yoshika has decided to change a couple of matters:

1. Smaller items of shop fittings and equipment would no longer be capitalised but, instead, written off as expenses.

2. The depreciation approach for larger items of equipment will be changed.

This decision was taken by Yoshika just before the annual winter holiday and so instructed Pat to make the appropriate adjustments.

Identify and explain five weaknesses in the general ledger system and explain the impact of each deficiency.

Weakness	Evaluation of impact

44 INVENTORY PURCHASES

Pat Singh, Healthyou's Deputy Managing Director, is concerned about the procedures that are in place in respect of inventory purchases, and has recently attended a fraud and money laundering event. Pat has asked you to review the following procedures:

Purchases

Healthyou has a list of trusted suppliers that it deals with regularly.

When supplies are needed, orders are placed with these suppliers by staff over the telephone. No order number is required to place an order.

Goods are left at the door of the warehouse by suppliers with no checks or records being updated at the point of delivery. Later on, a goods received note is completed, however it is common for items to be found as damaged or even missing. The goods received notes are filed together in the warehouse, and are kept in date order.

If the warehouse team find any short deliveries, they notify the accounts team. The warehouse keep all the relevant paperwork so that they can monitor if certain suppliers regularly make short deliveries or send faulty goods. In order to save the warehouse staff time, the accounts team will request a credit note for both these and any damaged goods. There are a number of ongoing disputes with suppliers about missing items and damaged goods.

The accounts department require the purchase invoices to be sent straight to them. Invoices are entered onto the accounting system by Accounts Payable Clerk, Bai Firminio. Before Bai pays the supplier, the aged payables report is checked against the supplier statements at the end of the month, to ensure that all invoices are on the system. The Finance Director is often busy, so Bai has a payment limit that allows authorisation of the bank payments below a certain amount.

If a part is needed urgently, one of the warehouse staff takes money from petty cash and collects the part from a local supplier to avoid disrupting production. All staff have access to the petty cash tin. Petty cash always reconciles with an acceptable difference, although staff often have to be chased for receipts.

(i) Identify TWO types of fraud that may occur within an organisation.

(ii) For each type of fraud identified, describe TWO circumstances from Healthyou Ltd's situation above that may allow the fraud to occur.

Type of fraud	Circumstances

45 INVENTORY PURCHASES

Healthyou Ltd purchases supplies from Happy Oats. Because the oats are sold at low prices, Happy Oats have a policy that only goods damaged on delivery can be returned.

Happy Oats advertises itself as the cheapest oat supplier in the area, and in order to keep costs down, it sources all of its oats from overseas suppliers who are not restricted by minimum wage regulations. Happy Oats also states that its fast manufacturing processes are achieved through minimisation of quality control checks.

You have recently discovered that Happy Oats, one of your suppliers, is the family business of Kazu Kumar, Healthyou's Purchasing Manager. Kazu has been placing most bulk oat orders with Happy Oats. Kazu thinks that it will be offering the best price for the oats because of the family connection. Sometimes deliveries are made to Kazu's home address as goods can be received more quickly.

(i) Identify THREE potential risks in the system outlined above.

(ii) Identify the potential implication of each risk identified.

(iii) Recommend an appropriate safeguard to minimise each risk.

Potential risk	Potential implication	Safeguard to minimise risk

PRACTICE QUESTIONS: SECTION 2

46 NON-CURRENT ASSETS

This task is about the monitoring of accounting systems and how they work in practice.

The Deputy Managing Director, Pat Singh, has raised a concern about the accuracy of the value of non-current assets shown in the financial statements. You have been asked to review the way in which non-current assets are recorded on acquisition and the system in place to identify disposals.

Purchase and recording of assets

Non-current assets with a value of £100,000 or above must be authorised by Yoshika Mane (Finance Director). All other assets are authorised by the departmental manager. For example, the Regional Operations Manager, Jun Khan, authorises the purchase of new delivery vans.

The delivery of new assets is arranged for a time when the departmental manager is available to check them. This ensures that all new assets are undamaged on receipt. At this stage, the departmental manager matches the purchase order to the goods received note before filing them for future reference.

Invoices received on delivery are passed to the Accounts Payable Clerk, Bai Firminio, to process and pay in accordance with the supplier's policies. Bai ensures that the invoices are entered into the accounting software. As the invoice has come from the departmental manager, Bai is confident that the invoice simply needs coding for entry into the accounting software.

The item is also recorded on the non-current asset register by the Financial Controller, Ping Alonso, who decides the appropriate method and rate of depreciation for the new asset.

Ping also checks that all assets are still in use each year. This check is completed around the same time as the year-end inventory count. After all non-current assets have been confirmed as still in use, Ping then calculates the deprecation based on the rate decided when the asset was initially purchased.

Disposal of assets

When an asset is sold, a sales invoice is raised and recorded by the General Accounts Clerk, Setsuna Reina. Ping Alonso then removes the asset from the non-current asset register, calculates the profit or loss on disposal, then prepares the journal to remove the asset from the financial statements.

(i) **Identify THREE weaknesses in the system for the accurate recording of non-current assets outlined above.**

(ii) Evaluate the impact that each of the weaknesses described in part (i) could have on the organisation.

47 RISK RATING

As an employee in the finance department of a growing health supplement retail company, you are responsible for maintaining the integrity of financial records.

With your knowledge from AAT training, you are aware of the importance of identifying and assessing fraud risks. You have been asked to create a fraud matrix for the company, considering the potential fraud risks in the scenarios provided.

Identify the appropriate rating for each of the situations given below.

Situation
The retail business has several physical store locations in addition to its online presence. The stores experience a variable customer footfall, peaking during January when customers are pursuing new year health resolutions. To manage this, the company hires additional temporary sales staff, often on short notice. These temporary hires are sometimes paid in cash due to the urgency and short time span of their contracts. The process for checking the backgrounds of these individuals is not always thorough due to the rapid hiring process.
In line with the company's ethos of expertise and customer service, staff across all departments were traditionally given comprehensive training on all products and systems, allowing flexibility in job roles. However, recent budget cuts have led to a new policy where only key personnel receive in-depth training, with others receiving only basic instruction.
The health supplement retail company has recently expanded its range of products to include exclusive high-value supplements which are stored in a new central warehouse before distribution to stores and online customers. The inventory system has not been updated to reflect the high-value of these new items, and access to the warehouse is not adequately controlled, with multiple staff members having the keys to the storage facilities. Additionally, there are no regular inventory checks scheduled to account for these high-value items.

Options

High
Medium
Low

48 MONITOR, REVIEW AND REPORT

After a meeting with Jun Khan, the Regional Operations Manager for Healthyou, you have identified a risk in the in-store inventory management process:

- **Risk of not checking health supplement product expiration dates**

    Supplements are not consistently checked for expiration dates before being placed on the shop shelves, leading to the potential sale of out-of-date products.

Outline how you can MONITOR, REVIEW and REPORT on the risk described.

Risk	Monitor	Review	Report

UNDERSTAND THE IMPACT OF TECHNOLOGY ON ACCOUNTING SYSTEMS

49 NON-FINANCE PROFESSIONALS

Complete the following statements.

The best way to present financial data to non-finance professionals within your organisation is through a (GAP 1). You should consider the user's needs: determine what they need to see and then aim to (GAP 2).

In order to check that the information you are presenting is in a suitable format for users to understand and interpret during the presentation, it is useful to (GAP 3). You should then ensure that someone with limited technical knowledge can give you (GAP 4).

Gap 1	✓
data dashboard	
pivot table	

Gap 2	✓
add interactive graphics	
eliminate clutter and distraction	

Gap 3	✓
check that you have given a definition for all the technical terms	
show it to someone who hasn't seen it before	

Gap 4	✓
a summary of the information contained within the presentation	
definitions for all the technical terms included in the presentation	

50 PASSWORDS

You have been asked to set up a new system of passwords for Healthyou's accounting system.

Which TWO of the following reduce the effectiveness of passwords?

	✓
Requirement that passwords are changed every two weeks.	
Users are allowed to choose their own passwords.	
Automatic lock-out after 3 failed attempts to access the system.	
Making the sharing of passwords a disciplinary offence.	
Displaying the password on the screen when entered.	

51 MACHINE LEARNING

Identify whether the following statements about machine learning are true or false.

	True	False
Machine learning is a useful audit tool.		
Machine learning cannot support multi-dimensional or multi-variety data.		
The use of machine learning to code raw data will improve the accuracy of the reports produced.		
Machine learning does not enable continuous improvement.		
Humans do not need to be involved in decisions made using machine learning.		
Machine learning predictive models can be used to forecast revenue.		

52 DATA ANALYTICS

Complete the following statement.

The reliance on algorithmic predictions when using data analytics to analyse a wide selection of data is a cause for...	Gap 1	...particularly if the outcome is then considered...	Gap 2

Gap 1	✓
accuracy concerns,	
ethical concerns,	

Gap 2	✓
biased and unfair.	
inaccurate and may be misleading.	

53 INFORMATION

The provision of information in a more appealing and understandable manner is often referred to as which of the below?

	✓
Artificial Intelligence.	
Cloud computing.	
Data visualisation.	
Data simplification.	

54 INFORMATION

Raj has been analysing trends in the reviews on social media for Healthyou's main product line. However, many inconsistencies have been noticed.

Which of the 4 Vs of big data may be causing this problem?

	✓
Volume.	
Variety.	
Velocity.	
Veracity.	

55 WORKING FROM HOME

Increasing numbers of Healthyou's staff are considering working from home, so you are reviewing the policy for data and asset security.

Identify which of the following are required for the security of finance data stored on your company laptop when working from home.

Statement	Required ✓	Not required ✓
Lock your screen if leaving your laptop unattended.		
Ensure data is stored on an encrypted hard drive.		
Ensure access to USB ports has been restricted.		

56 DATA VISUALISATION

Which of the following is a benefit of data visualisation for the finance function?

	✓
Weekly or monthly reporting will be produced on time.	
Improved data security.	
Improved fraud detection.	
Improved insight and understanding.	

57 CLOUD COMPUTING

Which of the following is a disadvantage of cloud computing?

	✓
Increased flexibility to working arrangements.	
More reliance on third party suppliers.	
Access to continually up to date software.	
Easier integration of systems.	

RECOMMEND IMPROVEMENTS TO ACCOUNTING SYSTEMS

CHANGES TO THE ACCOUNTING SYSTEM

58 SWOT ANALYSIS

What is a SWOT analysis?

	✓
It is a management method whereby an organization can assess major external factors that influence its operation in order to become more competitive in the market.	
It is an analysis framework that matches an organisation's goals, programmes and capacities to the environment in which it operates.	
It is a framework or tool used to analyse and monitor the macro-environmental factors that may have a profound impact on an organisation's performance.	

59 PESTLE ANALYSIS

What is a PESTLE analysis?

	✓
It is a management method whereby an organization can assess major external factors that influence its operation in order to become more competitive in the market.	
It is an analysis framework that matches an organisation's goals, programmes and capacities to the environment in which it operates.	
It is a framework or tool used to analyse and monitor the macro-environmental factors that may have a profound impact on an organisation's performance.	

60 PEST ANALYSIS

What is a PEST analysis?

	✓
It is a management method whereby an organization can assess major external factors that influence its operation in order to become more competitive in the market.	
It is an analysis framework that matches an organisation's goals, programmes and capacities to the environment in which it operates.	
It is a framework or tool used to analyse and monitor the macro-environmental factors that may have a profound impact on an organisation's performance.	

PRACTICE QUESTIONS: SECTION 2

THE EFFECTS OF CHANGES ON USERS OF THE SYSTEM

61 CHANGEOVER

The directors of Healthyou are considering updating the accounting system.

Yoshika Mane (Finance Director) is suggesting that the direct changeover method be adopted. However, Sam Shah (Managing Director) has argued that direct changeover is usually the highest risk alternative available.

Which TWO of the following controls can mitigate the risk of system failure during direct changeover?

	✓
Training.	
Testing.	
Check digits.	
System documentation.	
Data backup.	

62 INFORMATION SYSTEM CONTROLS

Management information system controls may be classified as 'security controls' or 'integrity controls'.

Identify the correct category for the following controls.

	Security ✓	Integrity ✓
Locked doors.		
Fire alarms.		
Passwords.		
Authorisation of data entry.		
Batch totals.		
Check digits.		
Reconciliation.		
CCTV.		

63 SALES ORDER PROCESSING

This task is about the analysis of internal controls with recommendations to improve whilst considering the impact on users.

You have been asked to carry out a review of Healthyou's sales order processing and make recommendations for improvement.

Your findings are below.

Background data

Sales are currently made to retail customers through shops, and commercial customers across the world. Although the overseas market is expanding, Healthyou would like to develop its online market following the recent development of an online platform.

The company feels that an increased online presence will improve its sustainability, alongside other measures, such as the implementation of LED and sensor lighting, upgraded building insulation, and the introduction of recycled packaging.

Sales and orders

Catalogues will all be produced electronically and are available on the website or can be sent to customers by email. The website has a comprehensive list of products and is up to date with items that are out of stock. The website also gives dates when the items are expected back into stock and estimated delivery times.

Orders can now be placed via the website or email. No other order methods are accepted.

New customers and new products

All new customers are given a credit limit of £500 and 14 days to pay while initial credit checks are completed.

Credit checks are completed by an agency and a suggested credit limit is given. Once a month, the credit limits are updated on the system by Kate Santiago, Credit Controller. When this is done, any customers who are over their credit limit are emailed to ask for an immediate payment.

As the market is increasingly competitive, a number of new bespoke products are being considered as this will potentially give access to a new market with few competitors.

PRACTICE QUESTIONS: SECTION 2

Complete a SWOT analysis for the procedures outlined above.

(i) Identify ONE strength, ONE weakness, ONE opportunity to improve the procedures, and ONE threat to the effectiveness in the procedures outlined above.

(ii) Explain how the strength benefits the organisation.

(iii) Based on the weakness identified in (i):
- Describe the potential damage this weakness could cause the organisation.
- State a potential remedy to address this weakness.

(iv) Based on the opportunity identified in (i):
- State one change that should be made to the procedure.
- Explain how this change would benefit the organisation.

(v) Based on the threat identified in (i):
- Explain how the threat could damage the organisation.
- Identify an action that could be taken to improve the risk.

(i)	Strength	(ii)	Benefit
(i)	Weakness	(iii)	Damage and remedy
(i)	Opportunity	(iv)	Change and benefit
(i)	Threat	(v)	Damage and action

64 PURCHASING SYSTEM REVIEW

This task involves assessing the efficiency of internal controls within the purchasing system and providing suggestions for enhancements, with consideration of the impact on stakeholders.

You have been tasked with conducting a thorough review of Healthyou's purchasing system and proposing areas for improvement.

Your findings are as follows.

Background data

Healthyou's purchasing primarily consists of sourcing organic health supplement products and general supplies for their various shop locations. With a continued emphasis being placed on sustainability, the company is seeking more suppliers that offer eco-friendly and ethically sourced materials.

The procurement process has recently been updated to include an automated approval workflow for purchase orders. This is to ensure that orders are consistent with budgetary constraints and sustainable sourcing policies.

Purchasing and suppliers

All suppliers must undergo a rigorous vetting process before being added to the approved supplier list, which is accessible through the company intranet.

The Purchasing Manager, Kazu Kumar is responsible for negotiating contracts and managing supplier relationships with their team members. Purchase orders are now generated through an automated system and sent electronically to suppliers. The system tracks orders from placement through to delivery and payment.

New processes and technology

In an effort to become more efficient, the company has implemented a new enterprise resource planning (ERP) system. This system is intended to integrate various business processes, including purchasing, inventory management, and finance, however full implementation has been slow. The ERP system does include a supplier portal where suppliers can directly update their information, access purchase orders, and submit invoices, which is already up and running.

Complete a SWOT analysis for the procedures outlined above.

(i) Identify ONE strength, ONE weakness, ONE opportunity to improve the procedures, and ONE threat to the effectiveness in the procedures outlined above.

(ii) Explain how the strength benefits the organisation.

(iii) Based on the weakness identified in (i):
- Describe the potential damage this weakness could cause the organisation.
- State a potential remedy to address this weakness.

(iv) Based on the opportunity identified in (i):
- State one change that should be made to the procedure.
- Explain how this change would benefit the organisation.

(v) Based on the threat identified in (i):
- Explain how the threat could damage the organisation.
- Identify an action that could be taken to improve the risk.

(i) Strength	(ii) Benefit
(i) Weakness	(iii) Damage and remedy
(i) Opportunity	(iv) Change and benefit
(i) Threat	(v) Damage and action

AAT: INTERNAL ACCOUNTING SYSTEMS AND CONTROLS

65 COST-BENEFIT ANALYSIS I

A Cost-benefit analysis (CBA) has also been produced to support other decisions that are being made on the continued expansion of Healthyou. Sam Shah (Managing Director) has heard the issues identified can be categorised into Social, Environmental and Corporate, or People, Planet, Profit. You have been asked to categorise these findings.

The following statements are the results of the CBA.

Identify the appropriate category for each of the following statements.

Statement	Social ✓	Environmental ✓	Corporate ✓
Ability to recycle waste materials.			
Reduced inventory levels resulting in reduced storage costs.			
Automation of production resulting in redundancies.			
Change of delivery method to use electric vehicles.			
Improved efficiencies following training staff resulting in cost savings.			

66 PESTLE

Sam Shah (Managing Director) is not familiar with PESTLE and has asked you to show which category is appropriate for the statements given below.

Identify the appropriate category for each statement from the PESTLE analysis findings.

Statement	Political ✓	Economical ✓	Social ✓	Technological ✓	Legal ✓	Environmental ✓
Initiative to reduce carbon footprint.						
Trade uncertainties in SMEs (small and medium-sized enterprises) as a result of changing legislation.						
Changes due to existing Government legislation such as digital tax reporting.						
Increased automation resulting in redundant admin tasks.						
Investment in low energy products.						

67 COST-BENEFIT ANALYSIS II

The Deputy Managing Director, Pat Singh, at Healthyou is exploring the possibility of expanding the business further to include a new range of vegan-friendly health supplements to meet the growing demand for these products.

Currently, the company uses a very basic system to manage inventory and sales data. However, Financial Controller, Ping Alonso has raised concerns that this system may be inadequate for handling the increased complexity and volume of data with the proposed expansion.

Following a detailed research process, Ping has found a specialised inventory and sales management software system called EcoTrack, specifically tailored for health supplement businesses, which could handle the increased data load. The cost of this research was £1,500.

To support the implementation of EcoTrack, the company would need to invest in training for the inventory management team, which includes you and three other colleagues, at a cost of £400 per person (per day), for a two day course. Additionally, EcoTrack comes with an annual licence fee of £9,000.

Pat is also considering the option to upgrade all computer systems within the company to support the new software, which would incur an annual cost of £75,000.

By implementing EcoTrack, the company expects to reduce waste due to improved inventory management, leading to an estimated annual saving of £20,000. Based on initial market research, the Commercial Manager, Clem Seddon, predicts that the new vegan-friendly supplement range could produce an additional annual profit of £150,000, a figure that they consider to be a cautious estimate.

(a) (i) Complete a financial cost-benefit analysis for the above proposal.

Costs	£
Benefits	£
(Net Cost)/Benefit (£)	

(ii) Identify SIX non-financial factors that should be taken into account as part of the cost-benefit analysis.

(iii) Recommend, with TWO reasons, whether or not the proposed investment should be made.

Section 3

ANSWERS TO PRACTICE QUESTIONS

ROLE AND RESPONSIBILITIES OF THE ACCOUNTING FUNCTION

THE ACCOUNTING FUNCTION

1 ETHICS

Which statement provides a definition of business ethics?

	✓
Business ethics is concerned with complying with the law in business situations.	
Business ethics is concerned with complying with the law and all relevant accounting regulations.	
Business ethics is concerned with making the most appropriate moral judgements in business situations.	✓
Business ethics is concerned with avoiding illegal transactions in business situations.	

Business ethics is concerned with complying with the law in business situations. (Incorrect because ethics goes beyond mere legal compliance).

Business ethics is concerned with complying with the law and all relevant accounting regulations. (Incorrect because it is not only about compliance with accounting regulations and the law).

Business ethics is concerned with making the most appropriate moral judgements in business situations. (Correct because this statement reflects the application of moral principles to business activities).

Business ethics is concerned with avoiding illegal transactions in business situations. (Incorrect as it is a narrow view of ethics focused only on illegality).

AAT: INTERNAL ACCOUNTING SYSTEMS AND CONTROLS

2 GOOD ETHICAL BEHAVIOUR

Which TWO statements are key features of good ethical behaviour?

	✓
Good ethical behaviour increases costs without any significant benefits to the organisation.	
Good ethical behaviour helps to enhance the reputation of the organisation.	✓
Good ethical behaviour helps to reduce the risk of problems arising in the organisation.	✓
Good ethical behaviour may result in an organisation becoming uncompetitive.	

Good ethical behaviour increases costs without any significant benefits to the organisation. (Incorrect because ethical behaviour often brings about long-term benefits).

Good ethical behaviour helps to enhance the reputation of the organisation. (Correct as a good reputation is often a result of ethical conduct).

Good ethical behaviour helps to reduce the risk of problems arising in the organisation. (Correct because ethical practices can prevent issues such as fraud).

Good ethical behaviour may result in an organisation becoming uncompetitive. (Incorrect because, while there might be short-term costs, the long-term benefits often outweigh them).

3 IMPORTANCE OF ETHICS

Why is good ethical behaviour within the accounting function important?

	✓
It ensures that the business will make a profit on its trading activities.	
It ensures that employees in the accounting function will not make errors when performing their work.	
It guarantees that the accounting records do not contain any errors omissions or misstatements.	
It helps to maintain the accuracy and reliability of the accounting records.	✓

It ensures that the business will make a profit on its trading activities. (Incorrect as ethics does not guarantee profit).

It ensures that employees in the accounting function will not make errors when performing their work. (Incorrect because mistakes can still happen, regardless of ethics).

It guarantees that the accounting records do not contain any errors, omissions, or misstatements. (Incorrect as it cannot guarantee the absence of errors).

It helps to maintain the accuracy and reliability of the accounting records. (Correct as ethics promotes honesty and diligence in maintaining records).

ANSWERS TO PRACTICE QUESTIONS: SECTION 3

4 SUSTAINABILITY

Which statement provides a definition of sustainability?

	✓
Sustainability is defined as minimising the financial cost of inputs to produce the required products and services.	
Sustainability is defined as meeting the needs of the present whilst minimising any adverse impact upon future generations to meet their own needs.	✓
Sustainability is defined as minimising waste and pollution when producing goods and services.	
Sustainability is defined as the business being able to continue in existence for as long as possible.	

Sustainability is defined as minimising the financial cost of inputs to produce the required products and services. (Incorrect as this definition focuses solely on cost reduction).

Sustainability is defined as meeting the needs of the present whilst minimising any adverse impact upon future generations to meet their own needs. (Correct as it captures the essence of sustainability).

Sustainability is defined as minimising waste and pollution when producing goods and services. (Incorrect as it is an aspect of sustainability but not a complete definition).

Sustainability is defined as the business being able to continue in existence for as long as possible. (Incorrect because it implies only longevity without considering environmental or social impacts).

5 GOOD SUSTAINABILITY PRACTICES

Which TWO of the following are good sustainability practices within the accounting function?

	✓
Having a paperless office, with employees using accounting software and email communication to do their work.	✓
Purchasing plastic office furniture as it is cheaper than wood and likely to last longer.	
Not installing double glazing on the office windows.	
Using video conferencing for meetings, rather than employees travelling to meet in person.	✓

Having a paperless office, with employees using accounting software and email communication to do their work. (Correct because it reduces the use of paper and the associated environmental impact).

Purchasing plastic office furniture as it is cheaper than wood and likely to last longer. (Incorrect because it does not consider the environmental impact of plastic production and disposal).

KAPLAN PUBLISHING

Not installing double glazing on the office windows. (Incorrect as double glazing can improve energy efficiency).

Using video conferencing for meetings, rather than employees travelling to meet in person. (Correct due to reduced travel and the associated environmental impact).

6 IMPORTANCE OF SUSTAINABILITY

Which TWO statements identify why an organisation should have good sustainability policies and practices?

	✓
Good sustainability policies and practices will ensure that the organisation will make a profit on its trading activities.	
Good sustainability policies and practices will always result in choosing the lowest cost when purchasing materials and other business inputs.	
Good sustainability policies and practices help to improve the long-term viability of the organisation.	✓
Good sustainability policies and practices help to maintain and improve the reputation of the organisation.	✓

Good sustainability policies and practices will ensure that the organisation will make a profit on its trading activities. (Incorrect as profitability is not directly guaranteed by sustainability).

Good sustainability policies and practices will always result in choosing the lowest cost when purchasing materials and other business inputs. (Incorrect as sustainability sometimes involves investing in more sustainable options).

Good sustainability policies and practices help to improve the long-term viability of the organisation. (Correct as they contribute to a sustainable business model).

Good sustainability policies and practices help to maintain and improve the reputation of the organisation. (Correct as they align with increasing consumer and stakeholder expectations).

ANSWERS TO PRACTICE QUESTIONS: SECTION 3

7 STAFF STRUCTURES I

Identify whether each of the following statements is true or false.

	True ✓	False ✓
A multinational organisation is likely to have a longer scalar chain than a single-site organisation.	✓	
A 'flat' organisation will have a long scalar chain.		✓
A manager in a 'flat' organisation will always have a narrower span of control than a manager in a 'tall' organisation.		✓
A manager's span of control may include employees who work in different departments or in different locations.	✓	

A multinational organisation is likely to have a longer scalar chain than a single-site organisation. (True because multinationals tend to have more levels of hierarchy/management).

A 'flat' organisation will have a long scalar chain. (False as flat organisations have fewer levels of hierarchy/management).

A manager in a 'flat' organisation will always have a narrower span of control than a manager in a 'tall' organisation. (False because in flat organisations, managers typically have a wider span of control).

A manager's span of control may include employees who work in different departments or in different locations. (True as modern management practices often involve overseeing diverse teams or employees based in different physical locations).

8 STAFF STRUCTURES II

Identify whether the following statements about a broad span of control are true or false.

	True ✓	False ✓
It improves productivity for the organisation.		✓
It has fewer levels of management.	✓	
It is less expensive to operate.	✓	
Employees can easily give feedback to managers on ways to improve systems.		✓

It improves productivity for the organisation. (False as a broader span of control can dilute focus and reduce the time spent on individual staff member supervision).

It has fewer levels of management. (True as it typically involves fewer layers of hierarchy/management).

It is less expensive to operate. (True because there are fewer management positions that require a salary to be paid).

KAPLAN PUBLISHING

AAT: INTERNAL ACCOUNTING SYSTEMS AND CONTROLS

Employees can easily give feedback to managers on ways to improve systems. (False as a broad span of control can limit the opportunities for individual feedback. A manager oversees a large number of employees which could mean the manager has less time for each employee to deliver feedback).

FINANCIAL INFORMATION USED BY STAKEHOLDERS

9 FINANCIAL INFORMATION I

Complete the following statements relating to financial information.

Monthly or quarterly accounts are normally prepared for the benefit of managers (GAP 1). These accounts help them to make decisions regarding controlling and managing the business (GAP2).

Picklist: GAP 1 business owners, potential investors, managers

Picklist: GAP 2 whether or not to invest in the business, controlling and managing the business

Explanation: The regular preparation of accounts allows managers to assess performance and make timely decisions regarding the control and management of the business.

10 ACCOUNTS PRODUCED BY MANAGERS

State whether the following statements are true or false.

	True / False
The form and content of accounts produced by managers for decision-making and control purposes must comply with the law and with relevant accounting standards.	False
Annual financial statements will contain exactly the same information as accounts produced by managers for decision-making and control purposes.	False

The form and content of accounts produced by managers for decision-making and control purposes must comply with the law and with relevant accounting standards. (False, because while external financial reports must comply with legal and accounting standards, internal management accounts are more flexible and tailored to management needs).

Annual financial statements will contain exactly the same information as accounts produced by managers for decision-making and control purposes. (False, because management accounts often contain more detailed and operational information that is not required in annual financial statements).

ANSWERS TO PRACTICE QUESTIONS: SECTION 3

11 FINANCIAL STATEMENTS I

Select which financial statement would enable a user to identify the information described.

	Financial statement
The amount of cash paid to purchase property, plant and equipment during the year.	Statement of cash flows
The amount of trade payables at the year end.	Statement of financial position
By how much the cash and equivalents balance has increased or decreased during the year.	Statement of cash flows
Whether or not land and buildings were revalued during the year.	Statement of changes in equity

Picklist: Statement of profit or loss, Statement of financial position, Statement of cash flows, Statement of changes in equity

The amount of cash paid to purchase property, plant, and equipment during the year. (Statement of cash flows, as it shows cash transactions related to investing activities).

The amount of trade payables at the year end. (Statement of financial position, as it shows the liabilities of the company at a given point in time).

By how much the cash and equivalents balance has increased or decreased during the year. (Statement of cash flows, as it reconciles the opening and closing balances of cash and equivalents).

Whether or not land and buildings were revalued during the year. (Statement of changes in equity, as it includes all changes in equity, not reported elsewhere such as revaluation surpluses).

AAT: INTERNAL ACCOUNTING SYSTEMS AND CONTROLS

12 FINANCIAL STATEMENTS II

State which financial statement will be used to identify information for the calculation of the following accounting ratios.

	Financial statement
Gearing ratio.	Statement of financial position
Gross profit margin.	Statement of profit or loss
Current ratio.	Statement of financial position

Picklist: Statement of profit or loss, Statement of financial position, Statement of cash flows, Statement of changes in equity

Gearing ratio. (Statement of financial position, as it requires information relating to debt and equity levels).

Gross profit margin. (Statement of profit or loss, as it is calculated using revenue and gross profit).

Current ratio. (Statement of financial position, as it compares current assets to current liabilities).

13 CEEDEE LTD

State whether or not each of the following situations would require Ceedee Ltd to make changes within its existing accounting systems.

	Change systems / No change
The directors decided to change the depreciation rate applicable to delivery vans.	Change systems
The recruitment of a new accounts clerk in the accounts department.	No change
The issue of an updated accounting standard dealing with the valuation of inventory.	Change systems

The directors decided to change the depreciation rate applicable to delivery vans. (Change systems, as the accounting system needs to reflect the change in depreciation calculation/rate.).

The recruitment of a new accounts clerk in the accounts department. (No change, as this is a staffing change and does not impact the accounting system itself).

The issue of an updated accounting standard dealing with the valuation of inventory. (Change systems, as the system must be updated to ensure that inventory valuation complies with the new standard).

ANSWERS TO PRACTICE QUESTIONS: SECTION 3

14 FINANCIAL INFORMATION II

State whether the following statements are true or false.

	True / False
Accounting information produced to assist decision making by managers is likely to be more detailed than the annual financial statements.	True
Annual financial statements contain all information that an external stakeholder would possibly need to make fully informed decisions.	False

Accounting information produced to assist decision making by managers is likely to be more detailed than the annual financial statements. (True, as management accounting information is often more granular to aid in decision making).

Annual financial statements contain all information that an external stakeholder would possibly need to make fully informed decisions. (False, as they may require additional information not included in the financial statements, such as market conditions or strategic plans).

15 PERFORMANCE INDICATORS

Identify the relevant component required as part of the calculation for each of the following performance indicators

Current ratio.	Gap 1
Inventory turnover.	Gap 2
Trade receivables collection period.	Gap 3
Return on capital employed.	Gap 4

Gap 1	✓
Total current assets	✓
Cost of sales	
Operating profit	
Revenue	

Gap 2	✓
Total current assets	
Cost of sales	✓
Operating profit	
Revenue	

Gap 3	✓
Total current assets	
Cost of sales	
Operating profit	
Revenue	✓

Gap 4	✓
Total current assets	
Cost of sales	
Operating profit	✓
Revenue	

Current ratio. (Total current assets, as it is calculated by dividing total current assets by total current liabilities).

Inventory turnover. (Cost of sales, as it is calculated by dividing cost of sales by inventory).

Trade receivables collection period. (Revenue, as it is calculated using the trade receivables balance divided by the revenue amount. This is then multiplied by 365 days, to provide a result in a number of days).

Return on capital employed. (Operating profit, as it is calculated using profit from operations divided by capital employed).

16 FINANCIAL INFORMATION III

Identify whether the following statements about financial information are true or false.

	True / False
The budgetary control report is presented to the board of directors.	True
The statement of financial position is used to determine the liquidity of an organisation.	True

The budgetary control report is presented to the board of directors. (True, as it is a key financial report used for strategic decision making).

The statement of financial position is used to determine the liquidity of an organisation. (True, as it shows the current assets and liabilities which are used to assess liquidity).

CHANGES TO MANAGEMENT INFORMATION

17 MANAGEMENT INFORMATION SYSTEMS I

State whether the following statements are true or false.

	True / False
It is not necessary for the management information system to distinguish between cash and credit sales when calculating the trade receivables collection period.	False
If the management information system is able to classify liabilities as either current liabilities or non-current liabilities, this provides useful financial information for both internal and external stakeholders.	True

It is not necessary for the management information system to distinguish between cash and credit sales when calculating the trade receivables collection period. (False, as the calculation specifically requires credit sales to measure how quickly receivables are being collected).

If the management information system is able to classify liabilities as either current liabilities or non-current liabilities, this provides useful financial information for both internal and external stakeholders. (True, as this classification is important for assessing short-term and long-term financial obligations).

ANSWERS TO PRACTICE QUESTIONS: SECTION 3

18   MANAGEMENT INFORMATION SYSTEMS II

Complete the following statements relating to management information systems.

When an organisation changes its strategic objectives, it will (GAP 1) require changes to its management information system. It is important that the management information system does (GAP 2) change to meet the needs of internal stakeholders.

Picklist: GAP 1 will, will not

Picklist: GAP 2 does, does not

Explanation: The management information system (MIS) must align with the organisation's current strategy at any given time. Internal stakeholders rely on the MIS for accurate and relevant information to make decisions.

EVALUATE INTERNAL CONTROL SYSTEMS

INTERNAL CONTROLS

19 ORGANISATION SIZE

State whether the following statements are true or false.

	True / False
A small organisation does not need to have any internal controls.	False
The accounting records in a large organisation which applies a range of effective internal controls in the accounting system will be guaranteed to be free from error.	False
An online retailer can apply a range of effective internal controls within its accounting software systems.	True

A small organisation does not need to have any internal controls. (False, even small organisations require internal controls to ensure financial accuracy, protect assets, and comply with laws and regulations. The absence of internal controls can lead to undetected financial mismanagement or fraud).

The accounting records in a large organisation which applies a range of effective internal controls in the accounting system will be guaranteed to be free from error. (False, no system of internal controls can provide an absolute guarantee of freedom from error. Internal controls help mitigate the risk of errors but cannot entirely eliminate it due to the potential for human error and system limitations).

An online retailer can apply a range of effective internal controls within its accounting software systems. (True, an online retailer can indeed implement effective internal controls within its accounting systems, such as automated checks, access controls, and regular audits to ensure financial transactions are accurately recorded and processed).

ANSWERS TO PRACTICE QUESTIONS: SECTION 3

20 TYPES OF INTERNAL CONTROL

Match the type of internal control with each of the control examples noted below.

	Type of control
An organisation operates a smartcard system with a barrier that prevents visitors accessing the building (other than reception area).	Physical
As part of the selection and recruitment process, an organisation requires that applicants undergo an aptitude test and provide confirmation of their academic qualifications.	Personnel
Within the accounts department of an organisation, Huan is responsible for recording cash receipts from credit customers, Kiran is responsible for updating the sales/receivables ledger accounts and Nilam performs the monthly reconciliation of the sales/receivables ledger control account with the total of the sales/receivables ledger balances.	Segregation of duties

Picklist: Authorisation and approval, Arithmetic and accounting, Supervision, Segregation of duties, Organisational, Physical, Personnel, Management

An organisation operates a smartcard system with a barrier that prevents visitors accessing the building (other than reception area). (A physical control as it involves securing the physical premises of the organisation and limiting access to authorised personnel only).

As part of the selection and recruitment process, an organisation requires that applicants undergo an aptitude test and provide confirmation of their academic qualifications. (A personnel control, as this relates to ensuring that the organisation hires qualified and suitable staff, which is essential for maintaining the integrity and effectiveness of operations).

Within the accounts department of an organisation, Huan is responsible for recording cash receipts from credit customers, Kiran is responsible for updating the sales/receivables ledger accounts, and Nilam performs the monthly reconciliation of the sales/receivables ledger control account with the total of the sales/receivables ledger balances. (Segregation of duties, which is a fundamental control to prevent fraud and errors. This example illustrates how the separation of responsibilities among different employees reduces the risk of incorrect or fraudulent activities).

21 TYPES OF INTERNAL CONTROL

Match the type of internal control with each of the control examples noted below.

	Type of control
An organisation requires that the purchase of any items of equipment which cost £500 or more is agreed in advance by a senior manager before the purchase is made.	Authorisation and approval
When starting a new job, Guang was presented with a job description which specified individual responsibilities and identified the departmental manager to contact if there were any work-related problems.	Organisational
Within the accounting and finance department of an organisation, Akira oversees the work of a new member of staff and is able to offer practical guidance and instruction to ensure that transactions are processed correctly.	Supervision

Picklist: Authorisation and approval, Arithmetic and accounting, Supervision, Segregation of duties, Organisational, Physical, Personnel, Management

An organisation requires that the purchase of any items of equipment which cost £500 or more is agreed in advance by a senior manager before the purchase is made. (Authorisation and approval controls are in place to ensure that significant expenditures are reviewed and approved by appropriate levels of management before the transaction occurs).

When starting a new job, Guang was presented with a job description which specified individual responsibilities and identified the departmental manager to contact if there were any work-related problems. (An Organisational control, where the structure of the organisation, including roles and reporting lines, is clearly defined to support effective management and control).

Within the accounting and finance department of an organisation, Akira oversees the work of a new member of staff and is able to offer practical guidance and instruction to ensure that transactions are processed correctly. (Supervision is a type of control activity that involves overseeing the work of others to ensure tasks are performed correctly and efficiently. This is essential, especially when training new staff or when complex tasks are undertaken).

22 EFFECTIVE INTERNAL CONTROLS

State whether the following statements are true or false.

	True ✓	False ✓
If a large multi-site organisation has comprehensive authorisation and approval procedures for transactions, along with effective segregation of duties in the accounting and finance department, it will still need a range of other internal controls to help manage organisational activities effectively.	✓	
An effective internal control system will prevent any fraud or error from occurring.		✓
In a small company with two directors and two employees in the accounting department it is still possible to have effective supervision and authorisation and approval controls in place.	✓	

If a large multi-site organisation has comprehensive authorisation and approval procedures for transactions, along with effective segregation of duties in the accounting and finance department, it will still need a range of other internal controls to help manage organisational activities effectively. (True, as while authorisation, approval, and segregation of duties are important, they are not the only controls needed. A robust system of internal control includes additional controls such as supervision, personnel, arithmetical and accounting, management and physical controls).

An effective internal control system will prevent any fraud or error from occurring. (False. An effective internal control system reduces the risk of fraud and error but cannot absolutely prevent it. There are always limitations to any control system, and some frauds or errors may still occur despite best efforts).

In a small company with two directors and two employees in the accounting department, it is still possible to have effective supervision and authorisation and approval controls in place. (True. Even in a small company, it is possible to establish effective controls. Supervision can be performed by the directors, and authorisation and approval controls can be structured to fit the size and complexity of the organisation).

AAT: INTERNAL ACCOUNTING SYSTEMS AND CONTROLS

23 RESPONSIBILITY FOR THE INTERNAL CONTROL SYSTEM

Within an organisation, who is responsible for ensuring that it has an effective system of internal controls?

	✓
The external auditor.	
The internal auditor.	
The board of directors.	✓
The finance director only.	

The external auditor. (Incorrect, as the external auditor's role is to provide an independent assessment of the effectiveness of internal controls as part of the audit process, not to ensure their implementation).

The internal auditor. (Incorrect, as the internal auditor evaluates the effectiveness of internal controls and provides recommendations for improvement, but the ultimate responsibility for the system of internal controls rests with the organisation's management).

The board of directors. (Correct, as the board of directors is ultimately responsible for the governance of the organisation, including ensuring that an effective system of internal controls is in place).

The finance director only. (Incorrect, as while the finance director plays a key role in the implementation and maintenance of internal controls within the financial domain, the responsibility for the overall system of internal controls is broader and includes the board of directors and senior management).

24 INTERNAL CONTROLS I

Match each of the following activities to the component that it illustrates.

	Control environment ✓	Information system ✓	Control activities ✓
Communication and enforcement of integrity and ethical values.	✓		
A requirement that all payments in excess of £1,000 require approval from two directors.			✓
The preparation of monthly management accounts.		✓	

Communication and enforcement of integrity and ethical values. (Control environment)
Explanation: The control environment is the foundation of all other components of internal control, providing discipline and structure. Communication and enforcement of integrity and ethical values are key elements of a strong control environment.

A requirement that all payments in excess of £1,000 require approval from two directors. (Control activities) Explanation: Control activities are the actions established through policies and procedures that help ensure management directives are carried out. Requiring dual approval for large payments is a control activity to prevent unauthorised or inaccurate transactions.

The preparation of monthly management accounts. (Information system) Explanation: The information system includes the methods and records that identify, assemble, analyse, classify, record, and report an entity's transactions and maintain accountability for the related assets and liabilities. The preparation of monthly management accounts is part of this system, ensuring management has accurate and timely financial information for decision making.

25 INTERNAL CONTROLS II

Match each of the following activities to the type of control that it illustrates.

	Authorisation and approval ✓	Arithmetical and accounting ✓	Physical control ✓
The purchase/payables ledger control clerk produces a reconciliation of the ledger account balances with the total on the payables ledger control account every month.		✓	
The petty cash float is kept in a locked box within a safe when not required.			✓
The chief accountant extracts a trial balance from the ledger accounts before preparing the annual accounts.		✓	

The purchase/payables ledger control clerk produces a reconciliation of the ledger account balances with the total on the payables ledger control account every month. (Arithmetical and accounting) Explanation: This is a control designed to ensure the arithmetical accuracy of the records. Reconciliation is a key accounting control that helps to verify the correctness and consistency of financial data.

The petty cash float is kept in a locked box within a safe when not required. (Physical control) Explanation: Physical controls are designed to secure and protect the assets of an organisation. Storing the petty cash in a locked box within a safe prevents unauthorised access and potential theft.

The chief accountant extracts a trial balance from the ledger accounts before preparing the annual accounts. (Arithmetical and accounting) Explanation: The preparation of a trial balance is an accounting control that checks the mathematical accuracy of the ledger accounts and ensures that debits and credits are equal before the final accounts are prepared.

26 INTERNAL CONTROLS III

Indicate whether the following limitations are true or false.

	True	False
If the costs of implementing a particular control exceed the benefits to be gained from its application, a business is unlikely to apply that control.	✓	
The effectiveness of many controls do not rely upon the honesty and integrity of individuals applying them.		✓
Internal controls apply to all items, irrespective of their value.	✓	
Standard controls are designed to deal with every possible transaction, no matter how unusual.		✓

If the costs of implementing a particular control exceed the benefits to be gained from its application, a business is unlikely to apply that control. (True. Cost-benefit analysis is an important consideration in the implementation of internal controls. If the cost of a control exceeds the benefits it provides, it may not be justifiable or practical to implement it).

The effectiveness of many controls does not rely upon the honesty and integrity of individuals applying them. (False, as while controls are designed to mitigate risks, their effectiveness often depends upon the honesty and integrity of the individuals involved. Controls can be avoided by collusion or management override).

Internal controls apply to all items, irrespective of their value. (True, in practice, it's important that controls are applied to every single item, regardless of the value).

Standard controls are designed to deal with every possible transaction, no matter how unusual. (False, as standard controls are designed to deal with routine transactions. Unusual or non-routine transactions may require specific controls tailored to the unique risks they present).

27 INTERNAL CONTROLS IV

Identify which control is suitable for each of the following weaknesses.

Weaknesses	Control
Theft of inventory from an open warehouse.	Gap 1
Purchase orders are sent to suppliers without attaching a Purchase Order number.	Gap 2
Entry of a one-off transaction into the accounting system.	Gap 3
Supplier accounts are managed and paid by the same person.	Gap 4
Incorrect entry of sales invoices into the sales daybook.	Gap 5
Non-compliance with appropriate accounting regulations and standards resulting from lack Of CPD.	Gap 6

Options	Gap No.
Management controls	Gap 3
Segregation of duties	Gap 4
Check arithmetical accuracy	Gap 5
Physical access controls	Gap 1
Authorisation and approval	Gap 2
Competent personnel	Gap 6

Theft of inventory from an open warehouse. (Physical access controls) Explanation: Physical access controls such as securing the warehouse with locks, surveillance systems, and restricted access areas help prevent theft of inventory.

Purchase orders are sent to suppliers without attaching a Purchase Order number. (Authorisation and approval) Explanation: Purchase Order numbers serve as an authorisation tool and allow for proper tracking and matching of orders. Without them, there is a risk of unauthorised purchases or duplicate orders being raised.

Entry of a one-off transaction into the accounting system. (Management controls) Explanation: Management controls would include procedures for reviewing and approving non-routine transactions to ensure that they are valid and correctly recorded.

Supplier accounts are managed and paid by the same person. (Segregation of duties) Explanation: Segregation of duties is a control that reduces the risk of error or fraud by dividing responsibilities among different individuals.

Incorrect entry of sales invoices into the sales daybook. (Check arithmetical accuracy) Explanation: Controls that check the arithmetical accuracy, such as regular reconciliations and reviews of the sales daybook entries, help to prevent and detect incorrect entries.

Non-compliance with appropriate accounting regulations and standards resulting from lack of CPD. (Competent personnel) Explanation: Ensuring that personnel have the necessary continuous professional development (CPD) is a control that maintains staff competency and adherence to accounting standards.

28 SMALL OR LARGE

Identify whether the following internal controls are more suitable for a small or a large organisation.

Internal control	Small	Large
Monthly inventory checks.		✓
Segregation of duties for the posting of purchase invoices, credit notes, preparing a supplier payment list and making payments to suppliers.		✓
All purchase orders must be authorised by the Managing Director.	✓	

Monthly inventory checks. (Large, as while any size organisation can benefit from inventory checks, larger organisations with more complex operations and higher volumes of inventory may find monthly checks more suitable to maintain accurate inventory records).

Segregation of duties for the posting of purchase invoices, credit notes, preparing a supplier payment list and making payments to suppliers. (Larger organisations are more likely to have the resources to segregate these duties among different employees, which helps prevent fraud and errors).

All purchase orders must be authorised by the Managing Director. (In smaller organisations, it may be practical for the Managing Director to review and authorise all purchase orders due to the limited number of transactions).

PREVENT AND DETECT FRAUD AND SYSTEMIC WEAKNESS

29 FRAUD I

Which TWO of the following would best reduce the risk of clothes being stolen from the store?

	✓
Segregation of duties between customer service staff on the shop floor and other members of staff taking payments from customers at tills.	
Requiring that all goods purchased are paid for by credit card or debit card, rather than cash.	
Each item of clothing has a security tag attached which can only be removed by a member of staff when the customer pays for the goods.	✓
In-store security guards and cameras monitor shoppers, particularly as they are leaving the store.	✓

Note: The question asks which statement would 'best' reduce the risk of clothes being stolen.

Segregation of duties between customer service staff on the shop floor and other members of staff taking payments from customers at tills. (Incorrect. This control is effective in reducing the risk of theft because it prevents one individual from having control over both the merchandise and the cash, reducing the opportunity for staff theft. However, this is not primarily focused on the risk of shoppers stealing the clothing items).

Requiring that all goods purchased are paid for by credit card or debit card, rather than cash. (Incorrect. While this may reduce some risks, it does not directly prevent clothes from being stolen. Therefore, it is not the best control for this specific risk).

Each item of clothing has a security tag attached which can only be removed by a member of staff when the customer pays for the goods. (Correct, as security tags are a physical control measure that can significantly reduce the risk of theft by triggering an alarm if someone attempts to leave the store with an unpaid item).

In-store security guards and cameras monitor shoppers, particularly as they are leaving the store. (Correct. The presence of security guards and cameras acts as both a deterrent and a means of detecting theft. They provide a physical presence that can monitor and respond to suspicious behaviour, which can effectively reduce the risk of clothes being stolen).

30 FRAUD II

Which TWO of the following control activities would best prevent this issue occurring?

	✓
The total cost of the payroll for the current month is compared with the total payroll cost for the previous month.	
All overtime claims must be reviewed and authorised by a manager prior to processing any payment.	✓
Review of working hours logged (e.g. by clock card, swipe card etc) by a responsible person.	✓
Supervision of the wages pay out by an independent official.	

Note: The question asks which control activities would 'best' prevent employee fictitious overtime claims occurring.

The total cost of the payroll for the current month is compared with the total payroll cost for the previous month. (Incorrect, as while this might highlight significant variances, it is not specific enough to detect fictitious overtime claims, as the total payroll cost could be influenced by other factors such as bonuses or salary changes).

All overtime claims must be reviewed and authorised by a manager prior to processing any payment. (Correct. Requiring managerial review and authorisation of overtime claims is a direct control that can prevent fictitious claims by verifying the legitimacy of the overtime worked before payment is made).

Review of working hours logged (e.g. by clock card, swipe card etc) by a responsible person. (Correct. By reviewing the actual logged hours, a responsible person can verify that the claimed overtime corresponds to the hours worked, thereby preventing fraudulent claims).

Supervision of the wages pay out by an independent official. (Incorrect. While supervision can be an effective control, it does not directly address the specific risk of fictitious overtime claims as it does not involve verifying the accuracy of the hours claimed).

AAT: INTERNAL ACCOUNTING SYSTEMS AND CONTROLS

31 FRAUD III

State whether the following statements are true or false.

	True	False
Fraud normally happens when someone has seen an opportunity, a weakness in the company's systems, and believes that the potential rewards will not outweigh the risk of being caught.		✓
The three prerequisites for fraud to occur are opportunity, motivation and honesty.		✓
Fraud investigations can often reveal a high level of inventory losses or unauthorised amounts written off to the sales/receivables ledger.	✓	

Fraud normally happens when someone has seen an opportunity, a weakness in the company's systems, and believes that the potential rewards will not outweigh the risk of being caught. (False. This statement is incorrect because it suggests that fraudsters believe the potential rewards do not outweigh the risks, which contradicts the general understanding that fraud occurs when individuals believe they can gain from exploiting a weakness without being caught or punished).

The three prerequisites for fraud to occur are opportunity, motivation and honesty. (False The correct statement should include 'opportunity, motivation, and rationalisation' rather than honesty. Honesty would prevent fraud, not facilitate it).

Fraud investigations can often reveal a high level of inventory losses or unauthorised amounts written off to the sales/receivables ledger. (True. Fraud investigations may uncover that inventory losses or write-offs to the sales/receivables ledger were not due to legitimate business reasons but were instead the result of fraudulent activities).

32 SYSTEMIC WEAKNESS

Identify the cause of the following weaknesses:

Weaknesses	Cause
Segregation of duties is deemed unnecessary.	Option 1
Management and supervision are based remotely.	Option 2
Staff create their own spreadsheets to prepare month-end reports instead of using Healthyou's accounting software.	Option 3
Inventory counts are rarely done.	Option 4

Option 1	✓
Lack of monitoring	
Lack of controls	✓
Lack of leadership	
Poor implementation of controls	

Option 2	✓
Lack of monitoring	
Lack of controls	
Lack of leadership	✓
Poor implementation of controls	

Option 3	✓	**Option 4**	✓
Lack of monitoring		Lack of monitoring	✓
Lack of controls		Lack of controls	
Lack of leadership		Lack of leadership	
Poor implementation of controls	✓	Poor implementation of controls	

Segregation of duties is deemed unnecessary. (Lack of controls. This weakness may arise from a lack of understanding of the importance of controls or from a belief that existing controls are sufficient when they are not, leading to an absence of segregation of duties).

Management and supervision are based remotely. (Lack of leadership. When management and supervision are not physically present, it can lead to a lack of leadership as employees may not receive the guidance and oversight they require).

Staff create their own spreadsheets to prepare month-end reports instead of using Healthyou's accounting software. (Poor implementation of controls. This weakness indicates that the existing controls related to the use of standardised accounting software are not being enforced, leading staff to use their own methods).

Inventory counts are rarely done. (Lack of monitoring. Infrequent inventory counts suggest a lack of ongoing monitoring processes to verify the accuracy and existence of inventory, which is a key control in preventing and detecting discrepancies).

33 FRAUD IV

Complete the following statements.

The financial statement area under scrutiny was inventories (GAP 1), where there was clear lack of controls (GAP 2).

The company has now mandated sequential purchase order numbering (GAP 3) to track orders effectively. This aims to enhance the integrity of the assets (GAP 4) reported.

Picklist: GAP 1 trade payables, inventories, revenue

Picklist: GAP 2 lack of controls, lack of leadership, lack of monitoring

Picklist: GAP 3 sequential purchase order numbering, an open-door policy with management, extended training of staff

Picklist: GAP 4 assets, income, equity

Explanation: When employees bypass the approval process for ordering materials, it indicates a lack of control over inventory management.

Site managers are available if employees have any queries, demonstrating leadership and monitoring is occurring.

Sequential purchase order numbering helps to track and control inventory levels, ensuring that assets are not overstated due to overstock and subsequent write-offs.

34 TYPES OF FRAUD

Identify whether the following are examples of non-financial or financial fraud.

	Non-financial	Financial
An employee falsified their qualifications and experience on their CV to secure a job role.	✓	
A cashier in a retail outlet deliberately under-scanned sales through the checkout, to allow friends to purchase items at a reduced price.		✓
Inventory theft from a central warehouse by delivery staff.		✓

An employee falsifying their qualifications and experience on their CV to secure a job is considered non-financial fraud. This form of deceit is related to the misrepresentation of personal credentials and capabilities. It does not directly involve the theft or misappropriation of company funds or assets. However, the implications can still be significant as it can lead to the company hiring someone who is not qualified for the position, potentially affecting the quality of the company's work/outputs.

A cashier who deliberately under-scanned sales through the checkout to allow friends to purchase items at a reduced price is an example of financial fraud. This action involves the manipulation of sales transactions for personal or third-party gain, resulting in a direct financial loss to the company.

Inventory taken from the central warehouse by delivery staff is considered financial fraud, as it directly affects the company's financial position. The stolen inventory represents company assets and these have been taken without permission.

ANSWERS TO PRACTICE QUESTIONS: SECTION 3

EVALUATE ACCOUNTING SYSTEMS AND PROCEDURES

EFFECTIVENESS OF THE ACCOUNTING SYSTEM

35 PURCHASE CYCLE CONTROLS I

Which TWO of the following controls in a purchase cycle could be implemented to reduce the risk of payment of goods not received?

	✓
Sequentially pre-numbered purchase requisitions and sequence check.	
Matching of goods received note with purchase invoice.	✓
Goods are inspected for condition and quantity and agreed to purchase order before acceptance.	✓
Daily update of inventory system.	

Sequentially pre-numbered purchase requisitions and sequence check. (Incorrect. This control helps ensure that all purchase requisitions are accounted for and that there is a systematic process for tracking them only).

Matching of goods received note with purchase invoice. (Correct, as this matching process verifies that the goods invoiced have been actually received, which is essential to prevent payments for undelivered goods).

Goods are inspected for condition and quantity and agreed to purchase order before acceptance. (Correct. Inspection of goods is important as it ensures the quality and quantity of goods received are accurate. It's also important to agree these details to the purchase order, before payments are made).

Daily update of inventory system. (Incorrect. Regular updates to the inventory system are important for accurate record-keeping but do not specifically address the risk of paying for goods not received).

36 PURCHASE CYCLE CONTROLS II

Which TWO of the following controls in the purchase cycle could be implemented to reduce the risk of procurement of unnecessary goods and services?

	✓
Centralised purchasing department.	✓
Sequentially pre-numbered purchase requisitions and sequence check.	
Orders can only be placed with suppliers from the approved suppliers list.	
All purchase requisitions are signed as authorised by an appropriate manager.	✓

Centralised purchasing department. (Correct. A centralised purchasing department can standardise procedures and oversight, reducing the risk of unnecessary or unauthorised purchases).

Sequentially pre-numbered purchase requisitions and sequence check. (Incorrect. While this control is important for tracking requisitions, it does not directly prevent the procurement of unnecessary goods and services).

Orders can only be placed with suppliers from the approved suppliers list. (Incorrect. This control ensures the use of reputable suppliers but does not necessarily prevent unnecessary purchases).

All purchase requisitions are signed as authorised by an appropriate manager. (Correct. Managerial authorisation provides a review process to verify that the goods and services requisitioned are necessary for the business before the purchase is made).

37 EXPENSE CLAIM CONTROLS

Which ONE of the following essential internal control measures is evidently missing?

	✓
Healthyou lacks a control environment as the board are not setting an ethical tone at the top.	✓
Healthyou lacks an Internal Audit department.	
Healthyou lacks an experienced finance manager.	
Healthyou lacks an external auditor.	

Healthyou lacks a control environment as the board are not setting an ethical tone at the top. (Correct. The control environment sets the tone for the organisation and influences the control consciousness of its people. The board's apparent acceptance of unethical expense claims suggests a deficient control environment).

Healthyou lacks an Internal Audit department. (Incorrect. While an internal audit function is important, the absence of one does not directly relate to the issue described, which is about the unethical manipulation of expense claims).

Healthyou lacks an experienced finance manager. (Incorrect. An experienced finance manager could help, but the root of the problem appears to be the board's attitude towards unethical behaviour, not necessarily the experience level of the finance manager).

Healthyou lacks an external auditor. (Incorrect. External auditors provide independent assurance, but their role does not directly address the day-to-day ethical tone set by the board or the internal control environment).

38 HEALTHYOU – INVENTORY COUNTING PROCESSES

Outline 3 weaknesses and their effect on the accounting systems in the boxes below:

Weakness	Effect of Weakness
The shop manager and staff should not be involved in the count at their own location.	It would be very easy for a member of staff to cover up a fraud – for example, had they stolen anything, then it would be easy to tick the pre-prepared inventory count sheet indicating the item was still on the premises. This would lead to an overvaluation of inventory.
The internal auditor should attend as an observer only and not have any involvement in the count itself. To do so confuses the roles of the people involved.	Errors in the process may not be detected as the internal auditor was busy "doing" rather than "observing". It is also possible that the internal auditor is not competent to recognise damaged or slow-moving inventory and so these items could go unrecorded.
The instructions are capable of being misinterpreted. When viewing loose items where customers can bring their own containers, it would be very difficult for staff to estimate the quantity.	Staff should not estimate qualities of 'loose' products, unless they have appropriate experience or training. This could lead to misstatement of the inventory values.

Note: this question only requested three weaknesses and effects. Other relevant answers may also be acceptable.

39 BANK RECONCILIATION

Which ONE of the following statements explains the purpose of a bank reconciliation?

	✓
It is a control to ensure that the bank statement balance as at the end of the accounting year is correct.	
It is a control to ensure that all payments required have been made.	
It is a control to minimise the risk of errors and omissions in the cashbook, and to identify such items for further investigation.	✓
It is a control to ensure that all unrecorded receipts are identified and recorded in the cashbook.	

It is a control to ensure that the bank statement balance as at the end of the accounting year is correct. (Incorrect, as the purpose of a bank reconciliation is not merely to confirm the bank statement balance but to reconcile it with the company's cashbook).

It is a control to ensure that all payments required have been made. (Incorrect, as a bank reconciliation is not specifically about confirming if all payments have been made. It is about ensuring all transactions are recorded correctly).

It is a control to minimise the risk of errors and omissions in the cashbook, and to identify such items for further investigation. (Correct. A bank reconciliation is performed to ensure that the cashbook reflects all transactions accurately and to identify discrepancies for investigation).

It is a control to ensure that all unrecorded receipts are identified and recorded in the cashbook. (Incorrect, because while identifying unrecorded receipts is part of the process, the bank reconciliation serves a broader purpose, which includes ensuring the accuracy and completeness of all transactions in the cashbook).

40 RECEIVABLES LEDGER CONTROL ACCOUNT RECONCILIATION

Which ONE of the following statements explains the purpose of the reconciliation of the trade receivables control account?

	✓
It is a control to ensure that receipts from credit customers have been accounted for.	
It is a control to ensure that invoices raised relating to credit customers have been accounted for.	
It is a control to ensure that entries in the control account agree with the total of the receivables ledger, which guarantees that there are no errors or omissions in either the control account or the ledger account balances.	
It is a control to ensure that entries in the control account agree with the total of the receivables ledger. Even if that's the case, the control account and/or ledger account balances may still contain errors or omissions.	✓

It is a control to ensure that receipts from credit customers have been accounted for. (Incorrect, as the purpose of the reconciliation is not limited to ensuring receipts are accounted for but encompasses all transactions).

It is a control to ensure that invoices raised relating to credit customers have been accounted for. (Incorrect, as while ensuring invoices are accounted for is important, the reconciliation process is about ensuring overall accuracy between the control account and the individual ledger account balances).

It is a control to ensure that entries in the control account agree with the total of the receivables ledger, which guarantees that there are no errors or omissions in either the control account or the ledger account balances. (Incorrect, as there is no guarantee that errors or omissions won't be present in either the control account or the ledger balance).

It is a control to ensure that entries in the control account agree with the total of the receivables ledger. Even if that's the case, the control account and/or ledger account balances may still contain errors or omissions. (Correct, as this is the opposite of the previous statement).

41 HERBUS SALES AND DESPATCH SYSTEM

Identify and explain FIVE deficiencies in Herbus' sales and despatch system and evaluate the impact of these deficiencies.

Deficiency	Evaluation of impact
Inventory availability for telephone orders is not checked at the time the order is placed. The order clerks manually check the availability later and only then inform customers if there is insufficient inventory available.	There is the risk that where goods are not available, order clerks could forget to contact the customers, leading to unfulfilled orders. This could lead to customer dissatisfaction, and would impact the firm's reputation.
Telephone orders are not recorded immediately on the three-part pre-printed order forms, these are completed after the telephone call.	There is a risk that incorrect or insufficient details may be recorded by the clerk and this could result in incorrect orders being despatched or orders failing to be despatched at all, resulting in a loss of customer goodwill.
Telephone orders are not sequentially numbered.	Orders could be misplaced whilst in transit to the despatch department, meaning that they will not be fulfilled. This will result in dissatisfied customers.
Customers are able to place online orders which will exceed their agreed credit limit by 10%.	This increases the risk of accepting orders from bad credit risks. If they default on payment, irrecoverable debts will need to be written off.
A daily pick list is used by the despatch department when sending out customer orders. However, it does not appear that the goods are checked back to the original order.	This increases the risk that incorrect goods are sent to customers, leading to customer dissatisfaction.
Additional staff have been drafted in to help the two sales clerks produce the sales invoices.	As the extra staff will not be as experienced as the sales clerks, there is an increased risk of mistakes being made when invoices are raised with customers being under or overcharged.
Discounts given to customers are manually entered onto the sales invoices by sales clerks. In addition, a clerk could forget to manually enter the discount or enter an incorrect level of discount for a customer.	This could result in unauthorised sales discounts being given as there does not seem to be any authorisation required. If the discount is not entered manually by the sales clerk, the sales invoice will be overstated and a loss of customer goodwill.

42 PAYROLL FRAUD

Identify which of the following procedures would detect the frauds identified above.

Procedures	Would detect ✓	Would not detect ✓
The Financial Controller performs a numerical accuracy check of all payslips.		✓
An online portal is used to send payslips directly to employees. A paper copy is not posted out to employees' home addresses.		✓
The payment list is prepared by Kim. Prior to any payment being made, this is reviewed, checked and authorised by the Financial Controller.	✓	
Zhong Salah (Payroll Manager) completes a check that ensures that all employees are paid (at least) the minimum wage.		✓
A wages control account is not maintained.		✓
Payslips are always prepared by Kim. These are then checked against bank payments by the Financial Controller.	✓	

The Financial Controller performs a numerical accuracy check of all payslips. This procedure would not detect the frauds as it checks only for calculation accuracy, not the validity of the payee or the amounts in relation to contractual payments.

An online portal is used to send payslips directly to employees. A paper copy is not posted out to employees' home addresses. This procedure would not detect the fraud as it relates to the method of distribution, rather than the accuracy or legitimacy of the payment information.

The payment list is prepared by Kim. Prior to any payment being made, this is reviewed, checked and authorised by the Financial Controller. This procedure would likely detect the fraud, as the Financial Controller would notice irregularities in the payment list, such as payments listed for non-employees.

Zhong Salah (Payroll Manager) completes a check that ensures that all employees are paid (at least) the minimum wage. This procedure would not detect the fraud since it focuses on compliance with minimum wage regulations, not the legitimacy of the payees or amounts paid.

A wages control account is not maintained. Failing to keep a wages control account could allow fraud to go undetected, due to a lack of proper reconciliation and monitoring.

Payslips are always prepared by Kim. These are then checked against bank payments by the Financial Controller. This procedure would detect the fraud as discrepancies between the payslips and actual bank payments would be identified by the Financial Controller.

43 HEALTHYOU'S GENERAL LEDGER SYSTEM

Identify and explain five weaknesses in the general ledger system and explain the impact of each deficiency.

Weakness	Evaluation of impact
There appears to be no approval required for any journal entries made by Yoshika, Ping or Pat.	This means that errors made in journals are much less likely to be discovered before the entry is made.
Access to the general ledger is given to under-qualified staff.	Pat is the HR director making it unlikely that this individual has a sound understanding of accounting issues. Specifically, it is unlikely that the change to the rules for non-current assets could be made correctly by someone without a thorough grasp of accounting rules. Errors could be made, deliberately or otherwise, in a crucial part of the accounting system.
General ledger accounts can be created without authorisation.	Irregular transactions could be hidden more easily in accounts created for fraudulent purposes.
A change to an accounting policy has been made by Yoshika without approval or consultation.	Accounting policies must be consistently applied and appropriate for the business. If changed, then adjustments may be required in comparative figures and an explanation of the reason for the change included in the financial statements.
The friendship between Yoshika and Ping could undermine the controls within the business. There is evidence of this already, as they do not review each other's journals due to the level of trust that exists between them.	Journals which are wrong, or for inappropriate purposes, will lead to misstatements in the annual financial statements. This may lead users to make inappropriate decisions based upon that information.

44 INVENTORY PURCHASES

(i) Identify TWO types of fraud that may occur within an organisation.

(ii) For each type of fraud identified, describe TWO circumstances from Healthyou Ltd's situation that may allow the fraud to occur.

Type of fraud	Circumstances
Theft OR Misappropriation of assets – physical.	Theft of cash from petty cash tin/unauthorised expenditure as there is no formal authorisation recording process for petty cash taken out of the tin. Goods ordered for personal use resulting from: • goods not being checked to order and GRN on arrival OR • no order numbers/lack of controls for placing orders. Theft of inventory before it is recorded as a result of goods being left unattended in warehouse.
False accounting OR Misappropriation of financial statements.	Incorrect recording of trade payables as there is: • no segregation of duties within the purchase ledger or • no authorisation of payments. Incorrect recording of invoices/payments as there is no segregation of duties for checking and posting invoices, statements and payments. Unsubstantiated credit note claims recorded in the purchase ledger as there is no formal control or authorisation of goods returns or requests for credit notes.

ANSWERS TO PRACTICE QUESTIONS: SECTION 3

45 INVENTORY PURCHASES

(i) Identify THREE potential risks in the system outlined above.

(ii) Identify the potential implication of each risk identified.

(iii) Recommend an appropriate safeguard to minimise each risk.

Potential risk	Potential implication	Safeguard to minimise risk
Collusion with supplier. OR Personal use items/goods ordered.	Loss of inventory as goods are delivered to home address.	Orders to be placed by a member of staff with no connection to the supplier. OR Orders to a connected supplier are approved by a director.
Reputational damage: poor quality, cheap goods.	Need to refund customers for poor quality goods. Expensive in relation to wastage. Sales negatively impacted, as associated with a supplier which uses cheap labour.	Review suppliers to make sure they are compliant with ethical practices/principles. Quality control procedures need implementing as a priority.
May not be best price as no alternatives considered.	Decreased profit. Costs too high.	Obtain more than one quote from potential suppliers.

46 NON-CURRENT ASSETS

(i) **Identify THREE weaknesses in the system for the accurate recording of non-current assets outlined above.**

> **Only three required**
>
> - No segregation of duties: invoices processed and paid by the same person.
> - Invoice not matched to goods received note (GRN) or purchase order (PO).
> - Managers authorise assets for their own department, with no apparent reference to budget or cash flow.
> - Authorisation limit is high.
> - Non-current asset register maintained and assets checked and adjusted by the same person.
> - Non-current asset calculations (depreciation, profit or loss on disposal) are not checked and may not be accurate.

(ii) **Evaluate the impact that each of the weaknesses described in part (i) could have on the organisation.**

> - Fictitious suppliers may be paid as no supporting paperwork is sent to the accounts department which may cause cash flow issues, as well as the recording of non-existent assets.
> - Assets delivered to departmental managers homes may not be discovered or there may be a delay, costly for the business and may cause cash flow issues.
> - Cash flow issues could arise where a series of uncoordinated, unbudgeted purchases are made, all authorised by different managers.
> - Non-current assets may be incorrectly recorded in financial statements as a result of very few checks completed throughout the financial year.
> - Financial statements will show an incorrect figure for non-current assets.
> - Disposal of non-current assets may be incorrectly recorded – cost, depreciation, profit or loss on disposal. Financial statements will show an incorrect figure for non-current assets.
> - Additions of non-current assets may be incorrectly recorded in the asset register, items missing or incorrect value, records will not reflect the actual assets held by the company.
> - Potential loss of, or identification of, unused non-current assets will not be identified for some time.
> - Incorrect depreciation methods or calculations used and will result in an incorrect profit figure being shown.

ANSWERS TO PRACTICE QUESTIONS: SECTION 3

47 RISK RATING

Identify the appropriate rating for each of the situations given below.

Rating	Situation
Option 1 High	The retail business has several physical store locations in addition to its online presence. The stores experience a variable customer footfall, peaking during January when customers are pursuing new year health resolutions. To manage this, the company hires additional temporary sales staff, often on short notice. These temporary hires are sometimes paid in cash due to the urgency and short time span of their contracts. The process for checking the backgrounds of these individuals is not always thorough due to the rapid hiring process.
Option 2 Medium	In line with the company's ethos of expertise and customer service, staff across all departments were traditionally given comprehensive training on all products and systems, allowing flexibility in job roles. However, recent budget cuts have led to a new policy where only key personnel receive in-depth training, with others receiving only basic instruction.
Option 3 High	The health supplement retail company has recently expanded its range of products to include exclusive high-value supplements which are stored in a new central warehouse before distribution to stores and online customers. The inventory system has not been updated to reflect the high-value of these new items, and access to the warehouse is not adequately controlled, with multiple staff members having the keys to the storage facilities. Additionally, there are no regular inventory checks scheduled to account for these high-value items.

Options

High
Medium
Low

KAPLAN PUBLISHING

AAT: INTERNAL ACCOUNTING SYSTEMS AND CONTROLS

48 MONITOR, REVIEW AND REPORT

Outline how you can MONITOR, REVIEW and REPORT on the risk described.

Risk	Monitor	Review	Report
Customers may purchase expired health supplements due to inadequate checks for expiration dates before re-stocking occurs.	How many shops are affected by this issue (it could be one shop, or various shops). Frequency of expired products found on shelves (during checks completed so far). Consider the volume of customer complaints of expired products. Look at sales data for any potential dips that could indicate customer dissatisfaction.	Internal audit/walk through test to identify additional controls needed. Conduct spot checks at different times to ensure compliance with business inventory rotation and date checking procedures.	Monthly report of out-of-date inventory items discovered. Chart/table showing inventory levels written off as unusable. Dashboard to display trends in expired product discoveries, highlighting areas for improvement.

ANSWERS TO PRACTICE QUESTIONS: SECTION 3

UNDERSTAND THE IMPACT OF TECHNOLOGY ON ACCOUNTING SYSTEMS

49 NON-FINANCE PROFESSIONALS

Complete the following statements.

The best way to present financial data to non-finance professionals within your organisation is through a (GAP 1). You should consider the user's needs: determine what they need to see and then aim to (GAP 2).

In order to check that the information you are presenting is in a suitable format for users to understand and interpret during the presentation, it is useful to (GAP 3). You should then ensure that someone with limited technical knowledge can give you (GAP 4).

Gap 1	✓
data dashboard	✓
pivot table	

Gap 2	✓
add interactive graphics	
eliminate clutter and distraction	✓

Gap 3	✓
check that you have given a definition for all the technical terms	
show it to someone who hasn't seen it before	✓

Gap 4	✓
a summary of the information contained within the presentation	✓
definitions for all the technical terms included in the presentation	

Gap 1: A data dashboard is an effective way to present financial data, as it provides an at-a-glance view of key metrics and performance indicators.

Gap 2: Eliminating clutter and distraction helps non-finance professionals focus on the most important information without being overwhelmed.

Gap 3: Showing the information to someone who hasn't seen it before helps to get a fresh viewpoint, to see if it is understandable to those without prior knowledge of the content.

Gap 4: Requesting a summary of the information contained within the presentation helps you judge whether non-finance professionals grasp the essential messages included within the presentation.

AAT: INTERNAL ACCOUNTING SYSTEMS AND CONTROLS

50 PASSWORDS

Which TWO of the following reduce the effectiveness of passwords?

	✓
Requirement that passwords are changed every two weeks.	
Users are allowed to choose their own passwords.	✓
Automatic lock-out after 3 failed attempts to access the system.	
Making the sharing of passwords a disciplinary offence.	
Displaying the password on the screen when entered.	✓

Requirement that passwords are changed every two weeks. (Incorrect). Frequently changing passwords is recommended for staff members using accounting systems.

Users are allowed to choose their own passwords. (Correct). This can reduce the effectiveness of passwords if users choose weak or commonly used passwords that are easy to guess or hack.

Automatic lock-out after 3 failed attempts to access the system. (Incorrect). This actually increases security by preventing repeated attempts by unauthorized users.

Making the sharing of passwords a disciplinary offence. (Incorrect). Discouraging password sharing increases security of the accounting system.

Displaying the password on the screen when entered. (Correct). This reduces the effectiveness of passwords because it could allow others to see the password as it is being entered.

51 MACHINE LEARNING

Identify whether the following statements about machine learning are true or false.

	True	False
Machine learning is a useful audit tool.	✓	
Machine learning cannot support multi-dimensional or multi-variety data.		✓
The use of machine learning to code raw data will improve the accuracy of the reports produced.	✓	
Machine learning does not enable continuous improvement.		✓
Humans do not need to be involved in decisions made using machine learning.		✓
Machine learning predictive models can be used to forecast revenue.	✓	

Machine learning is a useful audit tool. (True, as machine learning can analyse large datasets quickly and identify patterns that may indicate issues for auditors to investigate).

Machine learning cannot support multi-dimensional or multi-variety data. (False. Machine learning can handle complex, multi-dimensional and multi-variety data, which is one of its strengths).

The use of machine learning to code raw data will improve the accuracy of the reports produced. (True. Machine learning algorithms can process and code large volumes of raw data more consistently and accurately than humans).

Machine learning does not enable continuous improvement. (False. Machine learning algorithms can learn from new data and improve over time, which is a key aspect of continuous improvement).

Humans do not need to be involved in decisions made using machine learning. (False. Human oversight is crucial to interpret machine learning outcomes and make context-based decisions).

Machine learning predictive models can be used to forecast revenue. (True. Predictive models in machine learning can analyse historical data and identify trends to make revenue forecasts).

52 DATA ANALYTICS

Complete the following statement.

| The reliance on algorithmic predictions when using data analytics to analyse a wide selection of data is a cause for… | Gap 1 | …particularly if the outcome is then considered… | Gap 2 |

Gap 1	✓
accuracy concerns,	
ethical concerns,	✓

Gap 2	✓
biased and unfair.	✓
inaccurate and may be misleading.	

Gap 1: Algorithmic predictions can raise ethical concerns, especially if they are used to make decisions that affect people's lives.

Gap 2: If the algorithmic predictions are based on biased data or flawed assumptions, they may be considered biased and unfair, leading to unethical outcomes.

53 INFORMATION

The provision of information in a more appealing and understandable manner is often referred to as which of the below?

	✓
Artificial Intelligence.	
Cloud computing.	
Data visualisation.	✓
Data simplification.	

Artificial Intelligence (or AI). (Incorrect. AI refers to the simulation of human intelligence in machines).

Cloud computing. (Incorrect. Cloud computing refers to the delivery of computing services over the internet).

Data visualisation. (Correct. Data visualisation is the representation of information in graphical or pictorial form to make data more appealing, accessible and understandable).

Data simplification. (Incorrect. While related to making information more understandable, data simplification is not the term used to describe the visual representation of data that relates to it being more appealing).

54 INFORMATION

Which of the 4 Vs of big data may be causing this problem?

	✓
Volume.	
Variety.	
Velocity.	
Veracity.	✓

Volume. (Incorrect. Volume refers to the amount of data, not its consistency).

Variety. (Incorrect. Variety refers to the different types of data, not its consistency).

Velocity. (Incorrect. Velocity refers to the speed at which data is processed, not its consistency).

Veracity. (Correct. Veracity refers to the quality and accuracy of data, which would affect the consistency of reviews).

ANSWERS TO PRACTICE QUESTIONS: SECTION 3

55 WORKING FROM HOME

Identify which of the following are required for the security of finance data stored on your company laptop when working from home.

Statement	Required ✓	Not required ✓
Lock your screen if leaving your laptop unattended.	✓	
Ensure data is stored on an encrypted hard drive.	✓	
Ensure access to USB ports has been restricted.	✓	

Lock your screen if leaving your laptop unattended. This is a basic security measure to prevent unauthorised access. This means that other family members or home visitors cannot view or access company/confidential information.

Ensure data is stored on an encrypted hard drive. Encryption is a key security measure to protect sensitive data held on a laptop.

Ensure access to USB ports has been restricted. Restricting USB port access prevents unauthorised data transfers and other physical breaches relating to the laptop.

56 DATA VISUALISATION

Which of the following is a benefit of data visualisation for the finance function?

	✓
Weekly or monthly reporting will be produced on time.	
Improved data security.	
Improved fraud detection.	
Improved insight and understanding.	✓

Weekly or monthly reporting will be produced on time. (Incorrect. While data visualisation can aid in understanding important information, it does not inherently affect the timeliness of report production).

Improved data security. (Incorrect. Data visualisation does not directly impact data security measures).

Improved fraud detection. (Incorrect. Data visualisation can assist in identifying fraud patterns within a set of data, but it is not a direct benefit of the visualisation itself).

Improved insight and understanding. (Correct. Data visualisation helps users to better understand complex data through visual representation).

57 CLOUD COMPUTING

Which of the following is a disadvantage of cloud computing?

	✓
Increased flexibility to working arrangements.	
More reliance on third party suppliers.	✓
Access to continually up to date software.	
Easier integration of systems.	

Increased flexibility to working arrangements. (Incorrect. This is an advantage of cloud computing, as it allows for remote access to systems and data).

More reliance on third-party suppliers. (Correct. Utilising cloud services increases dependency on external providers, which can be a disadvantage if there are service disruptions or other issues).

Access to continually up to date software. (Incorrect. This is an advantage, as cloud services often include regular updates and maintenance).

Easier integration of systems. (Incorrect. This is also an advantage as cloud services are designed to be compatible with a variety of applications and systems).

… ANSWERS TO PRACTICE QUESTIONS: SECTION 3

RECOMMEND IMPROVEMENTS TO ACCOUNTING SYSTEMS

CHANGES TO THE ACCOUNTING SYSTEM

58 SWOT ANALYSIS

What is a SWOT analysis?

	✓
It is a management method whereby an organization can assess major external factors that influence its operation in order to become more competitive in the market.	
It is an analysis framework that matches an organisation's goals, programmes and capacities to the environment in which it operates.	✓
It is a framework or tool used to analyse and monitor the macro-environmental factors that may have a profound impact on an organisation's performance.	

It is a management method whereby an organization can assess major external factors that influence its operation in order to become more competitive in the market. (Incorrect. This description more closely aligns with PESTLE analysis, which focuses on external factors).

It is an analysis framework that matches an organisation's goals, programmes and capacities to the environment in which it operates. (Correct. SWOT analysis helps to identify Strengths, Weaknesses, Opportunities, and Threats related to business competition or project planning).

It is a framework or tool used to analyse and monitor the macro-environmental factors that may have a profound impact on an organisation's performance. (Incorrect for describing a SWOT analysis. A SWOT analysis is a strategic planning tool that is used to identify and analyze the internal Strengths and Weaknesses of an organisation, as well as the external Opportunities and Threats it faces. This framework helps organisations understand their strategic position and make informed decisions. It does not specifically focus on macro-environmental factors. That would be more applicable to a PESTLE analysis, which looks at the broader external environment including Political, Economic, Social, Technological, Legal, and Environmental factors).

AAT: **INTERNAL ACCOUNTING SYSTEMS AND CONTROLS**

59 PESTLE ANALYSIS

What is a PESTLE analysis?

	✓
It is a management method whereby an organization can assess major external factors that influence its operation in order to become more competitive in the market.	
It is an analysis framework that matches an organisation's goals, programmes and capacities to the environment in which it operates.	
It is a framework or tool used to analyse and monitor the macro-environmental factors that may have a profound impact on an organisation's performance.	✓

It is a management method whereby an organization can assess major external factors that influence its operation in order to become more competitive in the market. (Incorrect. This description is too general and can apply to various types of analyses).

It is an analysis framework that matches an organisation's goals, programmes and capacities to the environment in which it operates. (Incorrect. This description better fits a SWOT analysis).

It is a framework or tool used to analyse and monitor the macro-environmental factors that may have a profound impact on an organisation's performance. (Correct. PESTLE stands for Political, Economic, Social, Technological, Legal, and Environmental factors that can affect an organisation).

60 PEST ANALYSIS

What is a PEST analysis?

	✓
It is a management method whereby an organization can assess major external factors that influence its operation in order to become more competitive in the market.	✓
It is an analysis framework that matches an organisation's goals, programmes and capacities to the environment in which it operates.	
It is a framework or tool used to analyse and monitor the macro-environmental factors that may have a profound impact on an organisation's performance.	

It is a management method whereby an organization can assess major external factors that influence its operation in order to become more competitive in the market. (Correct. PEST analysis focuses on Political, Economic, Social, and Technological factors that can influence an organization).

It is an analysis framework that matches an organisation's goals, programmes and capacities to the environment in which it operates. (Incorrect. This is a general description that does not specifically relate to PEST analysis).

It is a framework or tool used to analyse and monitor the macro-environmental factors that may have a profound impact on an organisation's performance. (Incorrect. This description is more applicable to a PESTLE analysis which includes additional factors of Legal and Environmental).

ANSWERS TO PRACTICE QUESTIONS: **SECTION 3**

THE EFFECTS OF CHANGES ON USERS OF THE SYSTEM

61 CHANGEOVER

Which TWO of the following controls can mitigate the risk of system failure during direct changeover?

	✓
Training.	
Testing.	✓
Check digits.	
System documentation.	
Data backup.	✓

Training. (Incorrect. Training users on how to use the new system can reduce the risk of errors once the new system is fully up and running.)

Testing. (Correct. Thorough testing of the new system before going live can identify and resolve issues, reducing the risk of system failure).

Check digits. (Incorrect. Check digits are used for error detection in numerical data, not for mitigating risks during system changeovers).

System documentation. (Incorrect. While important, system documentation itself does not mitigate the risk of system failure during changeover).

Data backup. (Correct. Having data backups ensures that information can be restored in the event of a failure during the changeover process).

62 INFORMATION SYSTEM CONTROLS

Identify the correct category for the following controls.

	Security ✓	Integrity ✓
Locked doors.	✓	
Fire alarms.	✓	
Passwords.	✓	
Authorisation of data entry.		✓
Batch totals.		✓
Check digits.		✓
Reconciliation.		✓
CCTV.	✓	

Locked doors - This is a physical security control to prevent unauthorised access to sensitive areas.

Fire alarms are part of the physical security measures to protect assets and personnel from fire hazards.

Passwords are a key security control to prevent unauthorised access to systems.

Authorisation of data entry is an integrity control. Authorisation ensures that only valid and accurate data is entered into the system.

Batch totals are used to check the completeness and accuracy of data processing (an integrity control).

Check digits are used for error detection and correction in numerical data entry (an integrity control).

Reconciliation ensures that data is consistent and accurate across different records and systems (an integrity control).

CCTV is used for surveillance to enhance physical security.

63 SALES ORDER PROCESSING

Complete a SWOT analysis for the procedures outlined above.

(i) Identify ONE strength, ONE weakness, ONE opportunity to improve the procedures, and ONE threat to the effectiveness in the procedures outlined above.

(ii) Explain how the strength benefits the organisation.

(iii) Based on the weakness identified in (i):
- Describe the potential damage this weakness could cause the organisation.
- State a potential remedy to address this weakness.

(iv) Based on the opportunity identified in (i):
- State one change that should be made to the procedure.
- Explain how this change would benefit the organisation.

(v) Based on the threat identified in (i):
- Explain how the threat could damage the organisation.
- Identify an action that could be taken to improve the risk.

(i) Strength	(ii) Benefit
Able to maintain up to date inventory records OR Easy for all customers to place orders.	Customers will be able to place orders for available stock/inventory only, reduces waiting times and frustration of unknown waiting times for items that are out of stock.
(i) Weakness	(iii) Damage
Initial credit limit set and not updated quickly.	New customers may exceed their credit limit, which may increase irrecoverable debts. OR New customers may not be able to place orders for the full amount of goods they need so may lose potential new customers. OR Delay in updating credit limit and chasing debt may lead to irrecoverable debts occurring. OR May prevent new customers from placing larger orders. **Remedy** Immediate update to credit limits. Cash on delivery until credit checks are completed.
(i) Opportunity	(iv) Change
Improve the initial credit limit setting procedure, e.g. perform as a background website check when customers are placing an order.	Introduce the facility for an initial online credit check to be performed before giving the initial credit limit. **Benefit** Would reduce irrecoverable debts. Customers with good credit would be able to place larger orders.

AAT: INTERNAL ACCOUNTING SYSTEMS AND CONTROLS

(i) **Threat**	(v) **Damage**
Adverse market reaction to bespoke products.	May result in reputational damage.
	Loss of customers to competitors.
	Action
	Research current and potential customers to see if there is demand for bespoke products.

64 PURCHASING SYSTEM REVIEW

Complete a SWOT analysis for the procedures outlined above.

(i) Identify ONE strength, ONE weakness, ONE opportunity to improve the procedures, and ONE threat to the effectiveness in the procedures outlined above.

(ii) Explain how the strength benefits the organisation.

(iii) Based on the weakness identified in (i):
- Describe the potential damage this weakness could cause the organisation.
- State a potential remedy to address this weakness.

(iv) Based on the opportunity identified in (i):
- State one change that should be made to the procedure.
- Explain how this change would benefit the organisation.

(v) Based on the threat identified in (i):
- Explain how the threat could damage the organisation.
- Identify an action that could be taken to improve the risk.

(i) **Strength**	(ii) **Benefit**
Automated approval workflow for purchase orders.	Ensures spending is within budget and adheres to company policy, reduces risk of over-ordering and enhances sustainability efforts. OR
OR	
Rigorous vetting process for suppliers.	Careful vetting of suppliers is a way of controlling the quality of products purchased, cost efficiency and supply chain reliability.
(i) **Weakness**	(iii) **Damage**
Delays experienced in the ERP system integration/ implementation.	Delays could disrupt purchasing cycles, leading to stock-outs or excess inventory being held. OR
	Inefficient integration could lead to miscommunication with suppliers and errors in orders.

ANSWERS TO PRACTICE QUESTIONS: SECTION 3

	Remedy
	Allocate additional resources for ERP system roll-out, integration, training and support.
	Develop a contingency plan for purchases made during the integration phase.
(i) Opportunity	**(iv) Change**
Leverage the supplier portal for better communication and self-service.	Encourage suppliers to use the portal for real-time updates and invoice submissions.
	Benefit
	Improves accuracy of supplier information and streamlines the invoicing process, leading to quicker payment cycles and better supplier relationships.
(i) Threat	**(v) Damage**
Resistance to new processes from internal staff or suppliers.	May result in non-compliance with new procedures and underutilisation of the ERP system.
OR	**Action**
Potential new suppliers may be unwilling to use the new systems in place.	Implement comprehensive training programs and provide incentives for adherence to new processes.
Note: Credit may be awarded for other relevant reasonable answers.	

65 COST-BENEFIT ANALYSIS I

Identify the appropriate category for each of the following statements.

Statement	Social ✓	Environmental ✓	Corporate ✓
Ability to recycle waste materials.		✓	
Reduced inventory levels resulting in reduced storage costs.			✓
Automation of production resulting in redundancies.	✓		
Change of delivery method to use electric vehicles.		✓	
Improved efficiencies following training staff resulting in cost savings.			✓

Ability to recycle waste materials. – Environmental. This relates to the environmental benefits of reducing waste.

Reduced inventory levels resulting in reduced storage costs. – Corporate. This relates to the financial benefits for the company.

Automation of production resulting in redundancies. – Social. This relates to the impact on the workforce and employment.

Change of delivery method to use electric vehicles. – Environmental. This relates to the environmental benefits of reducing emissions.

Improved efficiencies following training staff resulting in cost savings. – Corporate. This relates to the financial benefits of increased productivity and efficiency.

66 PESTLE

Identify the appropriate category for each statement from the PESTLE analysis findings.

Statement	Political ✓	Economical ✓	Social ✓	Technological ✓	Legal ✓	Environmental ✓
Initiative to reduce carbon footprint.						✓
Trade uncertainties in SMEs (small and medium-sized enterprises) as a result of changing legislation.	✓					
Changes due to existing Government legislation such as digital tax reporting.					✓	
Increased automation resulting in redundant admin tasks.				✓		
Investment in low energy products.						✓

Initiative to reduce carbon footprint. – Environmental. This is related to the organisation's environmental impact and sustainability efforts.

Trade uncertainties in SMEs as a result of changing legislation. – Political. This refers to the impact of political decisions on the business environment. An actual change in legislation itself is considered to be a political factor.

Changes due to existing Government legislation such as digital tax reporting. – Legal. This refers to compliance with laws and regulations. When a change arises due to existing legislation that is already in place, it can either be a political or legal factor. In this case, it has been selected as a legal factor, due to the mention of both the government and tax reporting statutory requirements.

Increased automation resulting in redundant admin tasks. – Technological. This refers to the impact of new technologies on business processes.

ANSWERS TO PRACTICE QUESTIONS: SECTION 3

Investment in low energy products. – Environmental. This is related to the organisation's environmental sustainability and energy efficiency efforts.

67 COST-BENEFIT ANALYSIS II

(a) (i) **Complete a financial cost-benefit analysis for the above proposal.**

Costs	£
Upgrade computer system	75,000
Software licence costs	9,000
Training costs (4 people × 2 days × £400)	3,200
Benefits	**£**
Profit from new vegan-friendly products	150,000
Reduced waste saving	20,000
(Net Cost)/Benefit (£)	Benefit £82,800

(ii) **Identify SIX non-financial factors that should be taken into account as part of the cost-benefit analysis.**

Increased market share due to the introduction of vegan-friendly products.

Customer satisfaction with the availability of a wider range of health-conscious options.

Enhanced company image as a continued provider of eco-friendly and ethical products.

Staff motivation and morale boost due to working with advanced systems and expanded product lines.

Potential challenges in adapting to a new software system.

Training and development opportunities for staff leading to increased skills and job satisfaction.

Possible disruption to business operations during the transition to new software.

Market trends and consumer demand for vegan supplements.

Other relevant points may earn marks.

(iii) Recommend, with TWO reasons, whether or not the proposed investment should be made.

Recommendation:

Yes, the proposed investment should be made (own figure rule based on own calculations) because of the reasons below.

Reasons:

The significant net benefit shown in the cost-benefit analysis

Potential for growth in a niche market with high consumer demand for vegan products The projected increase in efficiency and reduction in waste through improved inventory management

Increased annual profits

OR

Recommendation:

No, the proposed investment should not be made (own figure rule based on own calculations) because of reasons below

Reasons:

Potential disruption and staff resistance during the transition to a new system

Uncertainties about long-term market trends and sustainability of demand for vegan supplements

Risk of unforeseen costs associated with the implementation of a new software system.

Note: Include recommendation and supporting explanation.

Section 4

MOCK ASSESSMENT QUESTIONS

Scenario

The tasks in this assessment are all based on the scenario of Silversmith Ltd (Silversmith).

Silversmith is an independent jewellery manufacturer and retailer. Following a period of rapid expansion, Silversmith has asked you, Safiya Bartelli, an Accounting Technician, to review the processes of the company and identify weaknesses in the internal controls that may have occurred due to the recent growth of the company.

Company background

History

Silversmith is a private limited company based in Harrogate which produces and distributes a range of silver jewellery.

The business began twelve years ago when Farah Silver started making silver earrings as a hobby. Farah was so successful that she decided to start a business, by obtaining premises and manufacturing an expanded range of jewellery.

She was joined by her cousin, Ben Smith, who had recently completed a Masters in Business Administration. Ben assumed responsibility for the administration of the business, allowing Farah to design and produce her own range of silver jewellery.

Farah and Ben decided to form Silversmith. They initially rented a large studio on an industrial estate in Harrogate, before expanding into a larger factory unit and warehouse on the same estate.

Recent developments

Silversmith has expanded rapidly over the last three years, through intense marketing activities and a successful online presence on popular social media sites. The company now employs several staff and has opened additional warehouses in Glasgow and Southampton.

In the last few months, the company has opened a second factory on its site in Southampton.

Silversmith has signed supply contracts with various high street retailers as well as continuing to supply independent stores. Retail customers are able to purchase direct from a factory shop at the Harrogate site.

Silversmith has also opened a number of small workshops in rented premises in a number of towns. These workshops, branded as Silversmith Studio, provide activity days where members of the public can make their own jewellery, as well as providing local retail outlets.

Ben has researched developments in the jewellery market and feels that Silversmith would be able to expand more quickly if it expanded its range beyond silver jewellery to include other forms of jewellery and giftware.

AAT: INTERNAL ACCOUNTING SYSTEMS AND CONTROLS

Resources

On 31 December 20X7, Silversmith had 72 employees.

Department	Number of staff
Manufacturing	15
Storage and distribution	26
Studio	10
Sales and marketing	8
Administration	8
Design and development	5

Most employees are based at the Harrogate site, which is where the majority of goods are produced. However, this site is now operating at capacity, so any additional production has been moved to Southampton.

This has led to increased costs for the company, so it is looking at alternative production processes to reduce costs, possibly including outsourcing.

Staff

Some of Silversmith's key personnel are listed below:

Managing Director	Farah Silver
Operations Director	Ben Smith
Finance Director	Emma Raducanu
Financial Controller	Leylah Fernandez
Credit Controller	Brian Jones
Accounts Payable Clerk	Joanne Harten
Accounts Receivable Clerk	Josh Pugh
General Accounts Clerk and Cashier	Jasmine Taylor
Payroll Clerk	Gloria Jones
Production Manager	Geva Mentor
Sales and Marketing Manager	Sanjay Patel
Warehousing Manager	Lee Johnson
Transport Manager	Karla Pretorius

Sustainability

The company has launched a comprehensive training programme for all employees, allowing it to ensure high standards of employee satisfaction, as well as workplace safety and productivity.

Environmentally, Silversmith has made a zero-carbon pledge to reduce carbon emissions (with an aim to becoming carbon negative). It is also keen to cut wastage with a view to financial savings. So far, this has included:

- reduced amounts of packaging for items delivered to customers
- amending the supplier approval process to focus on sustainability, through good working practices and fair pay
- increased levels of recycling
- automatic lighting via a sensor system.

TASK 1 (25 MARKS)

This task is about the purpose, structure and organisation of the accounting function.

You have been asked to review and develop a policy on ethics and sustainability for implementation over the next few years.

(a) (i) Identify whether each of the following would be a way to improve ethics and sustainability.

Statement	Would improve ✓	Would not improve ✓
Replace current plastic packaging with recyclable cardboard.		
Allowing a greater number of employees to park their cars on-site by re-painting the marked parking bays in the carpark.		
Switching production of jewellery abroad to improve profitability.		

(3 marks)

You are training Eliana, a new junior accountant who is joining your team. You feel that in order to provide the best training to Eliana, it is important that she understands organisational structure. Eliana has told you that she has recently studied the differences between tall and flat organisational structures.

(ii) Identify whether the following statements about a flat organisational structure are true or false.

Statement	True ✓	False ✓
A flat organisation has a long scalar chain.		
A flat organisation has fewer levels of management than a tall organisation.		
A flat organisation has a narrow span of control.		
A flat organisation is less expensive than a tall organisation.		

(4 marks)

Eliana has been learning about performance indicators as part of her training. She's still a little unsure about some of the calculations, so has asked you to identify what information from the financial statements is needed to calculate certain performance indicators.

(iii) Identify the relevant component required as part of the calculation for each of the following performance indicators.

Return on capital employed.	Gap 1
Gearing.	Gap 2
Operating profit margin.	Gap 3
Trade payables collection period.	Gap 4

Gap 1	✓
Gross profit	
Operating profit	
Non-current assets	
Non-current liabilities	

Gap 2	✓
Equity	
Finance costs	
Operating profit	
Non-current assets	

Gap 3	✓
Equity	
Trade receivables	
Revenue	
Cost of sales	

Gap 4	✓
Trade receivables	
Revenue	
Cost of sales	
Total current assets	

(4 marks)

In an effort to improve employees' work-life balance by reducing commuting time, Silversmith have started to allow non-production staff to work from home. Staff still need to ensure that appropriate data is maintained securely, with no breach of data security regulations. To assist in this process, Silversmith uses cloud accounting.

(b) (i) Identify whether the following statements relating to cloud accounting are true or false.

Statement	True ✓	False ✓
Remote working using cloud accounting will improve document accessibility.		
The use of cloud accounting will lead to increased hardware costs.		
The use of cloud accounting will mean that businesses are more likely to lose data.		
The use of cloud accounting means that data is always secure.		

(4 marks)

AAT: INTERNAL ACCOUNTING SYSTEMS AND CONTROLS

You have been working with Eliana to review Silversmith's data and operational security policy. Eliana has identified the following situations but is unsure which type of risk they represent.

(ii) Identify the correct risk for each statement below.

Statement	Risk
Farah had asked Gloria to send her the details of management salaries, but Gloria accidentally sent a group email to all Silversmith employees.	
During the recent hot weather, Henry, the office assistant, unplugged the main server in order to plug in a fan.	
Eliana discovered that Lee, the Warehousing Manager, has deactivated his antivirus software as it makes his laptop too slow.	
Eliana received an email that was apparently from a delivery service, telling her that they had tried unsuccessfully to deliver her parcel, and that she needed to click on a link to arrange re-delivery. Eliana did not think that she had ordered anything.	

Options
Loss of data
Data breach
Unauthorised remote access
Phishing

(4 marks)

As the levels of Silversmith's business have grown over the years, the volume of data processed has also significantly increased. The distribution of data depends on the level of management, each needing different levels of data. Eliana is unsure about these management levels and the appropriate type of data for each. You have produced a training document to assist Eliana, which includes a brief description of the different levels of management and the information that each level will use.

MOCK ASSESSMENT QUESTIONS: SECTION 4

(c) (i) Identify the information level corresponding to the described management roles within Silversmith.

Management role	
Farah Silver chairs any board meetings where Silversmith's long-term plans are discussed. The Sales and Marketing and Production Managers report their issues to Farah periodically at these meetings.	Gap 1
Lee Johnson is responsible for the day-to-day running of the Harrogate warehouse.	Gap 2
Geva Mentor is responsible for the assessment of performance and allocation of production resources to all locations.	Gap 3

Gap options	Gap No.
Operational level	
Tactical level	
Strategic level	

(3 marks)

(ii) Identify the correct information option that corresponds with the described information available within Silversmith

Data available	
Weekly production reports and staff shift pattern planner reports.	Gap 1
Annual stamping-machine utilisation percentage reports, and budget versus actual outputs per production unit.	Gap 2
Five-year profit or loss and cash flow forecasts, used to plan the timing of investments in machinery and potential new locations for Silversmith Studios.	Gap 3

Gap options	Gap No.
Tactical information	
Strategic information	
Operational information	

(3 marks)

AAT: INTERNAL ACCOUNTING SYSTEMS AND CONTROLS

TASK 2 (25 MARKS)

This task is about the types of fraud in the workplace combined with ways in which it can be detected and prevented.

In addition to its two manufacturing locations, Silversmith has many Silversmith Studios across the country, and three warehouses in Harrogate, Glasgow and Southampton. Due to the number of locations it is not possible for the senior management team to attend all the inventory counts, but local management have clear counting instructions and report back to head office.

Silversmith's warehouses are operational 24 hours a day, receiving raw materials from suppliers and despatching them to Silversmith's factories, as well as receiving finished goods from the factories before despatching them to customers and studios.

The company uses a courier service for all its outward deliveries. Due to low staffing levels, the couriers load the inventory into their vehicles themselves. When the courier arrives for a collection, the warehouse receptionist passes them the goods despatch notes (GDNs) and directs them to the appropriate area of the warehouse.

To ensure that inventory records are up-to-date, local staff perform regular inventory counts, and then make any necessary adjustments to the inventory records.

(a) Complete the following statements.

The above may result in the occurrence of ___GAP 1___ fraud, due to a ___GAP2___

In order to address this risk, Silversmith needs to implement ___GAP 3___ as soon as possible. This will ensure that the impact on ___GAP 4___ is minimised.

Gap 1	✓
misstatement of financial statements	
e-crime	
misappropriation of assets	

Gap 2	✓
lack of written instruction.	
lack of a risk matrix.	
lack of controls.	

Gap 3	✓
segregation of duties	
written instructions	
a series of physical controls	

Gap 4	✓
assets	
income	
liabilities	

(4 marks)

Ben Smith, Operations Director, observed that unfavourable discrepancies have been reported between budgeted and actual income, cash and inventory levels from the Silversmith Studios section of the business. Ben has conducted a review into the processes within the Silversmith Studios and discovered the following issues:

Customers can order jewellery through the Silversmith website for 'click and collect' at their local Silversmith Studio. Customer orders are stored in a small, unlocked storeroom at the back of the studio. Once customers have provided staff with a reference number for their order, the customers collect their package from the storeroom, and then return to the counter, where a member of staff confirms that the order number on the package matches the customer's order number.

Silversmith Studio retail customers pay with cash or card when buying jewellery. Each studio has an online till system to record sales and payments and issue refunds, together with a machine for card payments. Daily reconciliations of the till records to the cash takings and card machine receipts are performed by the studio manager once the studio has shut. The studios employ few staff and often studio managers serve customers when the studios are busy. The studios often have evening workshops, finishing late in the evening, so studio managers will sometimes take cash takings home before banking them the next day.

Customers can book workshops online via the Silversmith website or contact their local studio directly. Each workshop is run by a local freelance silversmith and focuses on a single type of jewellery, either earrings, rings, bracelets or necklaces. The studio can hold up to eight participants although no record is kept of attendees or the type of jewellery produced.

Deliveries of jewellery for resale and raw materials for the workshops are signed for by the studio managers. Inventory counts for each studio should be carried out on the last day of the month, after the studio has closed for the day. The studio managers are responsible for the count and then provide a monthly inventory report to head office. It has been reported that a number of studio managers actually perform the counts during the day to avoid staying late.

(b) (i) Identify FOUR weakness in the system that may result in fraud occurring. (4 marks)

(ii) Recommend an internal control for EACH weakness, giving a reason why it would help to prevent fraud. (8 marks)

Weakness that may result in fraud	Internal control to help prevent fraud	Reason it will help prevent fraud

AAT: INTERNAL ACCOUNTING SYSTEMS AND CONTROLS

You work as part of an Accounts department. During your AAT studies, you learned about recording fraud risk on a fraud matrix. You have discovered a number of potential areas where fraud could arise. You must complete a fraud matrix to assess the potential risks. The issues are described in the table below.

(c)   Identify the appropriate rating for each of the situations given below.

Situation
In the early days of the business, Farah and Ben handled their own bookkeeping requirements and a local accountancy firm in Harrogate prepared the accounts. As the business grew it became necessary to adapt, first by using the local firm's bookkeeping service, and then by creating Silversmith's own accounts department. This has been operating for a number of years and staff turnover is low. All staff in the department are either professionally qualified or studying towards a professional qualification. The business uses a well-established accounting software package, which is regularly reviewed and updated.
Silversmith are reviewing the payroll system and discover that there is a high turnover of staff, particularly in the Silversmith Studio sites. Silversmith Studio's staffing levels fluctuate between peak and off-peak seasons. As a result, many temporary staff are hired during peak times such as Christmas, and, due to time constraints, it is not always possible to take up formal employment references prior to employment. A number of these staff are paid in cash on a self-employed basis.
Silversmith is proud of its approach to training, and initially provided sufficient training to provide cover for holidays and sickness. As the business has become more cost-conscious, it has been decided to only train one person for each role.

Options

High
Medium
Low

(3 marks)

MOCK ASSESSMENT QUESTIONS: SECTION 4

You have discussed the system of ordering and accepting goods at the Glasgow warehouse with Lee Johnson, the Warehousing Manager. You have identified the following risk with this system:

- **Risk of accepting unauthorised, inaccurate or damaged deliveries**

    Goods are often delivered overnight, and are unloaded into a storage area adjacent to the warehouse. No system exists to check and record items as they are received and left in the storage area. Lee admits that deliveries often appear to be short or damaged.

(d) Outline how you can MONITOR, REVIEW and REPORT on the risk described. (6 marks)

AAT: INTERNAL ACCOUNTING SYSTEMS AND CONTROLS

TASK 3 (10 MARKS)

This task is about the effectiveness of internal controls.

Jasmine Taylor, General Accounts Clerk and Cashier, has approached you for some advice. She has suggested some internal controls, but wants to check that she fully understands what internal controls are and how they work. Jasmine has therefore asked you to check that her suggested controls are suitable for the purpose that she has identified, as she knows that you have recently completed your studies.

(a) Identify whether the following internal controls are suitable for the purpose given.

Internal control	Purpose	Is the internal control suitable? ✓
Pre-employment checks are completed for all new staff members prior to employment, and payments can only be made to staff on the payroll.	Compliance	Yes ☐ No ☐
All deliveries received must be checked to the supplier's delivery note, then checked against purchase order. Delivery note must be signed to acknowledge both checks.	Ensure quality internal and external reporting	Yes ☐ No ☐
Monthly supplier statement reconciliations performed by an accounts clerk and reviewed and signed by a responsible person.	Safeguard assets	Yes ☐ No ☐
Segregation of duties between authorisation and payment of supplier invoices.	Prevent and detect fraud	Yes ☐ No ☐

(4 marks)

MOCK ASSESSMENT QUESTIONS: SECTION 4

Following recent negative press surrounding UK textile factories using cheap labour, Farah and Ben are keen to publicise Silversmith's reputation for ethical behaviour. A review of the finance department identified that some of the systems in place do not promote ethical behaviours.

The following improvements to the system have been suggested to address this.

(b) Identify which of the following would promote ethical behaviour within an organisation.

Improvement	Promote ✓	Would not promote ✓
Working practices of all suppliers to be assessed prior to acceptance onto the approved supplier list.		
The purchasing policy permits the payment of bribes in countries where this is necessary to secure supply contracts.		
New starters must sign non-disclosure agreements preventing staff from posting negative comments about Silversmith on social media.		
In order to retain the services of senior managers, their annual bonuses are guaranteed.		
Every staff member has the ability to use two fully-paid days per annum to perform voluntary work, e.g. with a local charity		
Recruitment policies should ensure that vacancy shortlisting is carried out 'blind', i.e. without revealing any of the candidate's personal details.		

(6 marks)

TASK 4 (15 MARKS)

This task is about the monitoring of accounting systems and how they work in practice.

The current systems for high street retail outlet customers to place orders and for sales to be recorded are:

- Orders are placed using Silversmith's website (using customer log-ins).
- All orders are processed by the sales department. Order numbers are not required.
- All customers are given a 30-day credit account to encourage repeat business.
- Sales orders are passed to the supervisor of the nearest warehouse (Harrogate, Glasgow or Southampton) where they are packed ready for collection.
- Most orders are collected by a national courier, but some nearby customers prefer to collect their own goods to save time and delivery costs.
- On collection, couriers sign a goods despatched note (GDN) which is retained by the local warehouse supervisors to enable them to resolve any customer queries in respect of damage or shortage.
- Proofs of delivery (including mobile device photos where necessary) are provided by the courier to the warehouse supervisor, who stores them at the warehouse for reference. Any returned goods are placed back into the warehouse.
- No GDN or proof of delivery is obtained for those local customers who collect in person.
- Invoices are prepared by the accounts department and issued by the sales department once the goods are despatched. Josh Pugh, the Accounts Receivable Clerk, enters the invoices into the accounting system.
- At the end of each month Josh sends out customer statements.
- Josh opens the post each morning and banks any cheques received. Josh also reviews the online banking system for any direct credits from customers. Josh then enters the receipts into the accounting system, and to the relevant customer accounts.

(a) **Analyse the potential deficiencies in the system outlined above, together with their cause AND impact.** **(10 marks)**

AAT: INTERNAL ACCOUNTING SYSTEMS AND CONTROLS

The Finance Director, Emma Raducanu, has decided that a thorough review of the payroll system is needed. The last time a similar review was performed was 24 months ago. A number of the staff have said that there is little point in such a review, as most of the staff are the same, and the same controls are still in place.

(b) Complete the following statements.

The payroll department's internal controls need to be reviewed to ensure that	Gap 1	which may have occurred because…	Gap 2

Gap 1	✓
the internal control objectives are not irrelevant	
there are no dummy employees	

Gap 2	✓
of the low staff turnover.	
of changes in technology.	

(2 marks)

(c) Identify whether the following statements are true or false.

Statement	True ✓	False ✓
If management are able to override controls, this shows a weak control environment		
Lack of segregation of duties will always lead to fraud.		
The bank reconciliation is a type of internal control.		

(3 marks)

TASK 5 (25 MARKS)

This task is about the analysis of internal controls with recommendations to improve whilst considering the impact on users.

For this task, you are Jasmine Taylor, General Accounts Clerk and Cashier.

Silversmith is looking to continue to grow and Farah Silver (Managing Director) agrees with Ben Smith (Operations Director) that the best route to achieve this is through expanding their product range into other forms of jewellery and giftware.

The current system for costing a new jewellery product is a manual system. The limited range of jewellery currently produced has meant that up to now this manual system has been adequate. However, Emma Raducanu, the Finance Director, believes that there are increased risks of costing errors when using manual costings for an expanding range of products, especially given that Silversmith have never produced some of these items before.

Emma has commissioned research that identified the most suitable costing system for jewellery and giftware is one called JAGS. The cost of this research was £2,800.

You would need to attend a three-day training course at a cost of £500 per day. The Production Manager, Geva Mentor, would also need to attend the same course, along with two members of the production team.

The JAGS system would require new hardware to run it, so Farah has decided to upgrade all Silversmith's hardware to ensure maximum capacity and integration. As a result, there will be a cost of £124,000 per annum for the hardware. The annual licence fee for the software amounts to £14,000.

On reviewing the potential benefits of the new system you have identified that less overtime will be needed by both production and finance staff, with monthly management reports produced more quickly. The annual saving in overtime is likely to amount to £18,000.

A group of current high street retail customers were enthusiastic when shown the new range of products. Based on their response, Sanjay Patel, Sales and Marketing Manager, believes that these new products are likely to generate additional annual profit of £220,000, which he says is a conservative estimate.

(a) (i) Complete a financial cost-benefit analysis for the above proposal.

Costs	£
Benefits	£
(Net Cost)/Benefit (£)	

(6 marks)

(ii) Identify SIX non-financial factors that should be taken into account as part of the cost-benefit analysis.

(6 marks)

(iii) **Recommend, with TWO reasons, whether or not the proposed investment should be made.**

(3 marks)

As an additional task, and in preparation for the potential changes needed if the new system is introduced, you have also been looking at benefits of implementing a new information system.

(b) (i) **Identify which FOUR of the following would be considered to be intangible benefits of changing the information system.**

Benefit	✓
Improved customer service	
Quicker decision-making	
Savings in maintenance costs	
More time for strategic planning	
Reduced inventory levels	
Competitive advantage though lower costs	
Reduced staff overtime	
Better understanding of customer needs	

(4 marks)

(ii) Identify whether the following characteristics are associated with switching directly from the old system to a new system.

Characteristic	Associated ✓	Not Associated ✓
More expensive than alternative methods of implementation		
The business need not ensure that the new system is working perfectly before switching		
Eases the processing workload		
Increases the risk of an unsuccessful changeover compared to other methods		
Increases confidence in results from the new system		
Can sometimes represent the only possible solution		

(6 marks)

Section 5

ANSWERS TO MOCK ASSESSMENT QUESTIONS

TASK 1 (25 MARKS)

(a) (i) Identify whether each of the following would be a way to improve ethics and sustainability.

Statement	Would improve ✓	Would not improve ✓
Replace current plastic packaging with recyclable cardboard.	✓	
Allowing a greater number of employees to park their cars on-site by re-painting the marked parking bays in the carpark.		✓
Switching production of jewellery abroad to improve profitability.		✓

(3 marks)

(ii) Identify whether the following statements about a flat organisational structure are true or false.

Statement	True ✓	False ✓
A flat organisation has a long scalar chain.		✓
A flat organisation has fewer levels of management than a tall organisation.	✓	
A flat organisation has a narrow span of control.		✓
A flat organisation is less expensive than a tall organisation.	✓	

(4 marks)

KAPLAN PUBLISHING

(iii) Identify the relevant component required as part of the calculation for each of the following performance indicators.

Return on capital employed.	Gap 1
Gearing.	Gap 2
Operating profit margin.	Gap 3
Trade payables collection period.	Gap 4

Gap 1	✓
Gross profit	
Operating profit	✓
Non-current assets	
Non-current liabilities	

Gap 2	✓
Equity	✓
Finance costs	
Operating profit	
Non-current assets	

Gap 3	✓
Equity	
Trade receivables	
Revenue	✓
Cost of sales	

Gap 4	✓
Trade receivables	
Revenue	
Cost of sales	✓
Total current assets	

(4 marks)

(b) (i) Identify whether the following statements relating to cloud accounting are true or false.

Statement	True ✓	False ✓
Remote working using cloud accounting will improve document accessibility.	✓	
The use of cloud accounting will lead to increased hardware costs.		✓
The use of cloud accounting will mean that businesses are more likely to lose data.		✓
The use of cloud accounting means that data is always secure.		✓

(4 marks)

ANSWERS TO MOCK ASSESSMENT QUESTIONS: **SECTION 5**

(ii) Identify the correct risk for each statement below.

Statement	Risk
Farah had asked Gloria to send her the details of management salaries, but Gloria accidentally sent a group email to all Silversmith employees.	Data breach
During the recent hot weather, Henry, the office assistant, unplugged the main server in order to plug in a fan.	Loss of data
Eliana discovered that Lee, the Warehousing Manager, has deactivated his antivirus software as it makes his laptop too slow.	Unauthorised remote access
Eliana received an email that was apparently from a delivery service, telling her that they had tried unsuccessfully to deliver her parcel, and that she needed to click on a link to arrange re-delivery. Eliana did not think that she had ordered anything.	Phishing

Options
Loss of data
Data breach
Unauthorised remote access
Phishing

(4 marks)

(c) (i) Identify the information level corresponding to the described management roles within Silversmith.

Management role	
Farah Silver chairs any board meetings where Silversmith's long-term plans are discussed. The Sales and Marketing and Production Managers report their issues to Farah periodically at these meetings.	Gap 1
Lee Johnson is responsible for the day-to-day running of the Harrogate warehouse.	Gap 2
Geva Mentor is responsible for the assessment of performance and allocation of production resources to all locations.	Gap 3

Gap options	No.
Operational level	Gap 2
Tactical level	Gap 3
Strategic level	Gap 1

(3 marks)

KAPLAN PUBLISHING 117

(ii) Identify the correct information option that corresponds with the described information available within Silversmith

Data available	
Weekly production reports and staff shift pattern planner reports.	Gap 1
Annual stamping-machine utilisation percentage reports, and budget versus actual outputs per production unit.	Gap 2
Five-year profit or loss and cash flow forecasts, used to plan the timing of investments in machinery and potential new locations for Silversmith Studios.	Gap 3

Gap options	No.
Tactical information	Gap 2
Strategic information	Gap 3
Operational information	Gap 1

(3 marks)

ANSWERS TO MOCK ASSESSMENT QUESTIONS: SECTION 5

TASK 2 (25 MARKS)

(a) Complete the following statements.

The above may result in the occurrence of ___GAP 1___ fraud, due to a ___GAP2___

In order to address this risk, Silversmith needs to implement ___GAP 3___ as soon as possible. This will ensure that the impact on ___GAP 4___ is minimised.

Gap 1	✓
misstatement of financial statements	
e-crime	
misappropriation of assets	✓

Gap 2	✓
lack of written instruction.	
lack of a risk matrix.	
lack of controls.	✓

Gap 3	✓
segregation of duties	
written instructions	
a series of physical controls	✓

Gap 4	✓
assets	✓
income	
liabilities	

(4 marks)

(b) (i) Identify FOUR weakness in the system that may result in fraud occurring.

(4 marks)

(ii) Recommend an internal control for EACH weakness, giving a reason why it would help to prevent fraud.

(8 marks)

Weakness that may result in fraud. 1 mark per weakness. Max 4 marks. Marks not awarded for generic responses.	Internal control to help prevent fraud. 1 mark for internal control. Max 4 marks. Marks not awarded for generic responses.	Reason it will help prevent fraud. 1 mark for each. Max 4 marks.
Customers are unsupervised in the storeroom collecting package(s). (1)	Physical security over inventory/stock. (1) OR Storeroom should be locked. (1) OR Ensure customers are not left unsupervised. (1) OR Staff should collect package. (1)	Prevents theft/damage to inventory items. (1) OR Makes sure that items are kept secure and will not get damaged. (1)
Studio manager (SM) takes cash home. (1)	Reconciled cash takings to be banked in night-safe on the premises. (1) Cash sales to be discontinued, with card-only sales. (1) Banking runs should be completed by staff in pairs. (1)	This prevents later manipulation by SM (1) Removing opportunity for loss of cash, reduces the risk of theft/fraud by the SM. (1)

Workshop run by freelance silversmith (FS) with:	All workshop attendees to book online. (1) OR	Prevents unregistered attendees paying cash direct to FS. (1) OR
no record of attendees (1) OR	Inventory used in workshops to be signed out by FS, specifying type of jewellery, to allow reconciliation by SM. (1) OR	Prevents excess inventory being removed by FS/theft. (1)
type of jewellery. (1)		
Could result in:	SM to review workshop details to verify number of attendees and type of jewellery. (1)	
misappropriated cash from unrecorded attendees (1) OR		
loss of inventory due to more raw material being used than needed, excess removed by FS. (1)		
No segregation of duties for inventory:	Separate member of staff to perform count, countersigned by SM. (1)	Prevents misappropriation of inventory. (1)
SM signs for deliveries and performs inventory count. (1)		
SM provides the report to head office which they have completed the inventory count/supporting work for. (1)		
Inventory counts should be conducted after studio is closed (not during the working day). (1) OR	Retrain SM to ensure that all staff are aware that inventory counts must be performed after studio is closed. (1)	Operations Director can perform checks to ensure the counts are performed at the correct times. (1)
Performing inventory counts during opening hours increases the risk of theft/fraud occurring, as counts may be inaccurate and theft may not be noticed. (1)		

ANSWERS TO MOCK ASSESSMENT QUESTIONS: SECTION 5

(c) Identify the appropriate rating for each of the situations given below.

Rating	Situation
Option 1 Low	In the early days of the business, Farah and Ben handled their own bookkeeping requirements and a local accountancy firm in Harrogate prepared the accounts. As the business grew it became necessary to adapt, first by using the local firm's bookkeeping service, and then by creating Silversmith's own accounts department. This has been operating for a number of years and staff turnover is low. All staff in the department are either professionally qualified or studying towards a professional qualification. The business uses a well-established accounting software package, which is regularly reviewed and updated.
Option 2 High	Silversmith are reviewing the payroll system and discover that there is a high turnover of staff, particularly in the Silversmith Studio sites. Silversmith Studio's staffing levels fluctuate between peak and off-peak seasons. As a result, many temporary staff are hired during peak times such as Christmas, and, due to time constraints, it is not always possible to take up formal employment references prior to employment. A number of these staff are paid in cash on a self-employed basis.
Option 3 Medium	Silversmith is proud of its approach to training, and initially provided sufficient training to provide cover for holidays and sickness. As the business has become more cost-conscious, it has been decided to only train one person for each role.

Options

High
Medium
Low

(3 marks)

(d) Outline how you can MONITOR, REVIEW and REPORT on the risk described. (6 marks)

Risk	Monitor	Review	Report
No system to check and record items when delivered. Deliveries may: – include incorrect items/quantity of items – be damaged – be stolen prior to being transferred into the warehouse.	Warehouse Manager records volume of goods damaged on delivery. (1) Volume of theft of goods that are awaiting transfer to the warehouse (using delivery note matching). (1) Compare how much have been ordered and how much have been recorded. (1)	Check order against delivery note, invoice, PDB, PL, remittance and payment details. (1) Perform internal audit /walk through test to identify weaknesses where additional controls are necessary. (1) Purchase order matched to invoice. (1) Inconsistencies checked with supplier. (1)	Produce table/chart that shows potential shortages, loss of inventory. (1) Report of under/over inventory discovered on the count. (1) Produce table/chart that shows inventory written off due to damage. (1)

ANSWERS TO MOCK ASSESSMENT QUESTIONS: SECTION 5

TASK 3 (10 MARKS)

(a) Identify whether the following internal controls are suitable for the purpose given.

Internal control	Purpose	Is the internal control suitable? ✓
Pre-employment checks are completed for all new staff members prior to employment, and payments can only be made to staff on the payroll.	Compliance	Yes ✓ No
All deliveries received must be checked to the supplier's delivery note, then checked against purchase order. Delivery note must be signed to acknowledge both checks.	Ensure quality internal and external reporting	Yes No ✓
Monthly supplier statement reconciliations performed by an accounts clerk and reviewed and signed by a responsible person.	Safeguard assets	Yes No ✓
Segregation of duties between authorisation and payment of supplier invoices.	Prevent and detect fraud	Yes ✓ No

(4 marks)

(b) Identify which of the following would promote ethical behaviour within an organisation.

Improvement	Promote ✓	Would not promote ✓
Working practices of all suppliers to be assessed prior to acceptance onto the approved supplier list.	✓	
The purchasing policy permits the payment of bribes in countries where this is necessary to secure supply contracts.		✓
New starters must sign non-disclosure agreements preventing staff from posting negative comments about Silversmith on social media.		✓
In order to retain the services of senior managers, their annual bonuses are guaranteed.		✓
Every staff member has the ability to use two fully-paid days per annum to perform voluntary work, e.g. with a local charity	✓	
Recruitment policies should ensure that vacancy shortlisting is carried out 'blind', i.e. without revealing any of the candidate's personal details.	✓	

(6 marks)

TASK 4 (15 MARKS)

(a) Analyse the potential deficiencies in the system outlined above, together with their cause AND impact. (10 marks)

Deficiencies
- No customer order number
- Orders are not matched to invoices or delivery notes
- Credit given to potentially non-creditworthy customers
- No signed collection notes for local customers
- Accounts department do not have signed delivery proofs
- Potential for deliveries not to be invoiced
- Accounts are not aware of returned or damaged goods
- Josh has full responsibility for recording of invoices, cash received and statements.

Causes
- Lack of mandatory order numbers for all orders
- No credit checks performed before allowing credit
- Lack of formal procedure for collection of goods
- Lack of formal procedure to ensure that all orders are recorded and invoiced
- Lack of formal system for recording returns or damaged goods
- Lack of segregation of duties.

Impact
- Orders may be sent incorrectly
- Invoices may be for the incorrect goods and/or amount
- Potential theft by employees – may create fake accounts as no credit checks done
- Potential theft by employees – may steal cash, then issue credit notes to cover theft
- Poor relationship with/loss of customers due to invoice/credit note disputes
- Unrecorded sales – orders/delivery/invoices all completed separately

Other relevant points may be considered.

(b) Complete the following statements.

| The payroll department's internal controls need to be reviewed to ensure that | Gap 1 | which may have occurred because… | Gap 2 |

Gap 1	✓
the internal control objectives are not irrelevant	✓
there are no dummy employees	

Gap 2	✓
of the low staff turnover.	
of changes in technology.	✓

(2 marks)

(c) Identify whether the following statements are true or false.

Statement	True ✓	False ✓
If management are able to override controls, this shows a weak control environment	✓	
Lack of segregation of duties will always lead to fraud.		✓
The bank reconciliation is a type of internal control.	✓	

(3 marks)

ANSWERS TO MOCK ASSESSMENT QUESTIONS: SECTION 5

TASK 5 (25 MARKS)

(a) (i) Complete a financial cost-benefit analysis for the above proposal.

Costs	£
Hardware costs	124,000
Software costs	14,000
Training costs (4 people × 3 days × £500)	6,000
Benefits	**£**
Profit from new products	220,000
Overtime saving	18,000
(Net Cost)/Benefit (£)	Benefit £94,000

(6 marks)

(ii) Identify SIX non-financial factors that should be taken into account as part of the cost-benefit analysis.

> 1 × mark for reference to any points below: max 6 marks
>
> Enhanced reputation of Silversmith as major supplier of broader range of jewellery and giftware.
>
> Staff satisfaction at removal of the manual system.
>
> Staff satisfaction at reduced working hours, improving work-life balance and reputation as an ethical employer.
>
> Staff dissatisfaction at lack of overtime.
>
> Speedier production of reports.
>
> Faster decisions on whether to proceed with production of a new product.
>
> Improvement in staff morale as they see increased investment levels.
>
> Potential difficulties in switching to new system.
>
> Time taken to use system efficiently (learning curve)
>
> Other relevant points may earn marks.

(6 marks)

(iii) Recommend, with TWO reasons, whether or not the proposed investment should be made.

1 × mark for recommendation: 2 marks for supporting explanation – max 3 marks

Recommendation:

Yes, the proposed investment should be made (OFR based on own calculations) because of reasons below (1)

Reasons:

Enhanced reputation (1)

Increased revenue (1)

Reduced overtime costs (1)

Cost-benefit analysis shows net benefit (1)

Improved speed of costing (1)

Improved speed of reporting (1)

Enhanced ethical reputation due to reduced working hours (1)

OR

Recommendation:

No, the proposed investment should not be made (OFR based on own calculations) because of reasons below (1)

Reasons:

Cost-benefit analysis shows net cost (OFR) (1)

Staff unrest – reduced overtime (1)

Staff unrest – fear of change (1)

Difficulty changing system (1)

Staff may not be able to use the new system (1)

(3 marks)

(b) (i) Identify which FOUR of the following would be considered to be intangible benefits of changing the information system.

Benefit	✓
Improved customer service	✓
Quicker decision-making	✓
Savings in maintenance costs	
More time for strategic planning	✓
Reduced inventory levels	
Competitive advantage though lower costs	
Reduced staff overtime	
Better understanding of customer needs	✓

(4 marks)

(ii) **Identify whether the following characteristics are associated with switching directly from the old system to a new system.**

Characteristic	Associated ✓	Not Associated ✓
More expensive than alternative methods of implementation		✓
The business need not ensure that the new system is working perfectly before switching		✓
Eases the processing workload	✓	
Increases the risk of an unsuccessful changeover compared to other methods	✓	
Increases confidence in results from the new system		✓
Can sometimes represent the only possible solution	✓	

(6 marks)